This Book will meet a real need. It is evangelistic and realistic. Profound issues are handled with impressive simplicity . . . but it is never superficial. It reads like the communication of someone who meets you personally for a chat about what your life means. Many will find it extraordinarily helpful.

> *Rev. Donald English*
> *General Secretary*
> *The Methodist Church*

Peter Vardy has succeeded in clarifying profound philosophical and theological issues in a way that will help many honest enquirers with questions about God's reality and the meaning of life. This book would also be good reading for Christians who tend to avoid deep thought about the nature and implications of their faith. I warmly commend it.

> *Rev. Bernard Green*
> *General Secretary*
> *Baptist Union of Great Britain*

'. . . a robust account of the challenge and promise of Christian discipleship.'

> *Professor Colin Gunton*
> *Kings College, London*

An excellent and unusual book. Dr Vardy has provided a fascinating life that transcends the ut in any way minimalising o is both God and Man.

As Dr Vardy tianity requires passion and

> *Graham Leonard*
> *Bishop of London*

In this attractive and unusual book a layman who is also a philosopher presents the case for Christian faith in the language of any intelligent couple whose dinner conversation takes a serious turn. Wholly orthodox, but refreshingly free from the clerical tone of voice, his argument raises questions as well as answering them, and ends with a surprising twist that the conversation must go on after the book has ended.

Bishop John Taylor

And is it true? And is it true?
This most tremendous tale of all?
Seen in a stained glass window's hue,
A baby in an ox's stall?
The Maker of the stars and sea
Become a child on earth for me?

And is it true? For if it is,
No loving fingers tying strings
Around those tissued fripperies,
The sweet and silly Christmas things,
Bath salts and inexpensive scent
And hideous tie so kindly meant,

No love that in a family dwells,
No carolling in frosty air,
Nor all the steeple swinging bells
Can with this single Truth compare –
That God was Man in Palestine
And lives today in Bread and Wine.

John Betjeman

And if it's True?

Peter Vardy

Marshall Pickering

Marshall Morgan and Scott
Marshall Pickering
1 Beggarwood Lane, Basingstoke, Hants RG23 7LP, UK

Copyright © 1988 Peter Vardy
First published in 1988 by Marshall Morgan and Scott Publications
Ltd
Part of the Marshall Pickering Holdings Group
A subsidiary of the Zondervan Corporation

ISBN: 0 551 01763 5

Text Set in Baskerville by Input Typesetting Ltd
Printed in Great Britain by Cox & Wyman, Reading

Contents

Dedication

To

That Solitary Individual

Acknowledgements

Many of the ideas lying behind this book and some of the examples have their origins in the writings of Sören Kierkegaard. Reading suggestions are given at the back.

I am grateful to students from Heythrop and King's Colleges and Masters degree students from the Institute of Education (University of London) with whom I have had many helpful and enjoyable discussions about the various matters discussed here. Sarah Allen, Anne Baker and Paul Nicholson SJ as well as my wife, Anne, helped by reading drafts of the manuscript.

My thanks are due to the Roman Catholic community of Heythrop College, the largely Jesuit-run College of London University where I lecture; to members of the various Anglican churches in the Torridge group of parishes – in particular my 'home' church of Sheepwash; to the Baptists and Methodists in our area of North Devon with whom we work closely and well – with little sense of division between us – and also to individual Quaker friends who have added their own insights. All these have helped me to understand what a Christian community can and should be.

Lastly, without the literary midwifery of Christine Whitell, this book would not have been written. I shall always be grateful to her.

PETER VARDY
Heythrop College,
London
and
St. Clair, Devon

Advent 1987
to
Easter 1988

The Beginning

He: *I think I'll have the fish. What about a drink?*
She: *I'll have a lime juice please. The chicken looks interesting.*

It is 7.00 pm. Two people are enjoying a meal in a London pub. The tide is on the turn and the Thames lies below, placid and still, whilst the green and red lights of a loaded barge wink by. The bar is full – office workers having one for the road before they catch their trains home. The atmosphere is convivial at the end of a long and busy day. The couple's talk wanders over various issues as is the way when friends meet – career, family, holidays, the new car, the latest computer developments or the current amusing political story. Dinner continues and the crowd in the bar thins. The main course is completed and the friends decide that their waist-lines will sanction a dessert. Conversation begins to languish and one of the friends turns to a more serious note.

It is a familiar enough story, repeated up and down the country. The serious questions are there for all of us, but we seldom come across others with whom we can discuss them or who might be interested in the issues. Even among friends, it is common for one person not to really know what the other thinks about the central questions in life. 'Why are we here?'; 'What is life about?'; 'Is there a God?';

'What difference does it make if there is?'; 'What is religion about?'

If the discussion between the two friends becomes serious, one might admit to belief in God and even say that she is a Christian. If these beliefs are not shared, the very mention of words like 'God' and 'religion' can cause embarrassment. Politics, women and religion are, after all, the three issues banned from discussion in the officers' mess. If embarrassment does not stop the conversation, then over coffee the issue may be explored further. What is the difference between good men like Socrates, Gandhi and Jesus? What effects should there be in an individual's life if he says that he believes in God? What real difference does it make? From the outside, it seems to be largely a matter of going to church once a week, singing hymns and trying to 'be good' and, surely, the last of these is possible without the first?

Talking about the 'big questions' is often entertaining, enjoyable and guaranteed to raise the passions. Deciding, as an individual, where one stands is not easy. To go further and to analyse the consequences of any stand is more difficult still. Hardest of all is living out one's beliefs, wherever these may be.

Before either of the friends can think about how to live, they must first be clear on the options. It may well be that, when one of the friends has thought matters through, he will come to believe in God when previously he considered there was 'nothing in it' whilst, on the other hand, his friend who thought herself a Christian may only begin to realise that the demands of love are very great indeed if they are taken seriously.

Coolly, and without the heat that after dinner drinks can sometimes engender, let us explore these issues together. Even the individual who claims to be a Christian often avoids thinking through just what belief in God involves. Too often the radical challenge that Jesus proclaimed is transmuted. Christianity becomes a matter of carols at

Christmas, the crib with 'little Jesus meek and mild', Easter eggs, happy hymns and low-level demands. The reality is different – Christianity requires passion and commitment. Suffering and misunderstanding may lie along the road. There is, of course, an overwhelming positive benefit. The Christian who has truly found the love of God will find a peace, security and happiness which nothing else can bring, but the road to a relationship with God can be a stony one.

We are free, we can make our own choices. We are embarked on the sea of life and choose we must – we have no alternative. Choices about our lives cannot be avoided as a refusal to think, and a refusal to choose is, in itself, a choice. At the least, however, we should consider the consequences of the available options before the choices are made.

Socrates and Jesus

He: *I admit Jesus was a good man, but so were many other religious and moral leaders. Look at Gandhi!*

She: *Yes I agree, but there is a difference.*

Socrates and Jesus were both good men. They both tried to bring people to see a different way in which life could be lived, they both suffered opposition and they rejected the approach to life taken by most people in their societies. They were both brought to trial on false charges and were sentenced to death. Both could have escaped, but chose not to do so. The parallels are remarkable. If Christianity is true, however, then there must be some difference between these two.

*

Socrates lived in Athens between 470 and 399 B.C. Just inland from the city, in the mountains of southern Greece, lay the Delphi oracle. The oracle proclaimed that Socrates was the wisest man in Athens. Socrates could not understand this when he was told about it, as he felt that he knew nothing. He therefore set out to prove the oracle wrong by questioning those who were reputed to be wise. He questioned politicians, orators, skilled tradesmen and businessmen to find out the basis for their knowledge. All, when they were really pushed by his questions, revealed that they really knew very little. Their lives had no real basis and they had not thought through the way they were living or what the consequences were. They had accepted views and opinions handed down to them by the society in which they lived without thinking through the issues for themselves.

Socrates' questioning made people angry as, when their ignorance was revealed, they were made to look foolish in the eyes of the young men who followed Socrates.

Socrates finally came to the conclusion that the oracle was, in effect, saying that the wisest man was he who admitted his own ignorance. He developed the philosophic technique of teaching by means of question and answer (the so-called 'Socratic method'). He asked people questions and brought them to see things for themselves. The young people of Athens flocked to him, and their fathers strongly disapproved. Instead of accepting what their parents told them, the young people began questioning the values and lives of their parents.

What had appeared to many people in Athens to be clearly 'good' or 'bad' came to be seen as not as clear as many had first assumed. Indeed all the things that seemed so important to most people – power, influence, money, success and reputation – came to be seen as passing and of little worth.

The older generation eventually reacted. Socrates wanted people to see the value of a good life. The virtuous life, he showed, was much more in the interests of each person than the quest for money, power, reputation or material prosperity. Indeed it was better to suffer harm than to inflict it. Someone who is harmed physically by another may be in pain and may even, in the last analysis, be put to death – but his soul, which Socrates believed survived death, cannot be harmed by physical injury. The person who inflicts physical harm, on the other hand, is hurting his true self most of all.

When Socrates' young followers began to ask questions

of their parents, whose lives were largely based on self-interest, the parents became uncomfortable, then angry and, finally, they reacted. No one likes to be made to look foolish in front of the younger generation and the Athenian upper and middle classes were no exception.

In today's world, it is as if the British public and grammar schools taught pupils to question their middle-class parents about the basis of their lives. The young people did this to such good effect that the parents came uncomfortably close to seeing that their lives might have been based on a mistake.

Socrates was brought to trial on the twin charges of being an atheist and corrupting the young. The charge of atheism is a very old one. The early Christian martyrs were condemned to death on a charge of atheism. They were held to be atheists because they did not believe in the Roman gods. So, similarly, Socrates was accused of not believing in the Athenian gods. He did not accept the charge. Socrates firmly believed in a life after death and that the life each person lived on earth would determine what happened to the soul after death. To be sure, he did sometimes make fun of the picture of the 'Gods' portrayed by the Athenian priests – but it was the priests and the established religion he was mocking. The second charge of 'corrupting the young' was, however, more serious.

The charges against Socrates carried the death penalty and he had to defend himself before the assembled free citizens of Athens. The normal practice, when someone was accused on a serious charge, was for the accused to hire skilled orators who would flatter and persuade the citizens so that they granted an acquittal. Socrates, however, had no time for these professional orators. They were one of the groups of people who thought themselves wise, but whom Socrates had shown, by his questions, had very little knowledge of what life was about, the difference between good and evil or, indeed, most of the really important questions in life. They were like politicians –

excellent at appearing popular but often with little personal depth. He also thought that there was something dishonest in resorting to flattery to gain an acquittal. The laws of Athens should decide his guilt or innocence and this should be a matter of fact, not of which side had the better speakers.

When the 'Sharpeville Six' were under sentence of death in South Africa after being convicted of murder (even though there had been no evidence at their trial linking them directly to the killing, except that they had been part of the crowd when the murder took place), they demanded 'justice not mercy'. Socrates might have used the same words.

Socrates, therefore, refused the offers of his friends to hire persuasive speakers to defend him and instead conducted his own case. He argued the issues in a straight-forward way – coolly and logically showing that he was innocent of the charges. We have a record of his speech at the trial written by Socrates' friend and pupil, Plato (see *The Last Days of Socrates*, Penguin). Socrates' defence seemed absolutely water-tight, and under Athenian law, he was clearly innocent. His prosecutors, however, were trained speakers and used all the tricks and clever techniques of their trade to persuade the Athenians that Socrates was guilty. Many Athenians had been made to look foolish by Socrates and had had their values challenged – he was not a popular figure. He argued that he had done nothing wrong, but he was convicted.

Under Athenian law, Socrates could have suggested a sentence such as banishment from the city or a heavy fine and the Athenian assembly might have imposed the sentence instead of the death penalty. His friends tried to get him to do this. They even offered to pay the fine. Socrates, however, would not agree. He was innocent and if he had suggested an appropriate penalty he would be accepting his guilt. True, he might have avoided death, but he considered that living, and dying, by his convictions was more important. He was, therefore, sentenced to death: the sentence was to be carried out by him being required to take hemlock.

He talked to his friends before he died and, again, we have a record of the conversation. His friends wanted him to escape (which would have been easy) but, once again, he did not believe that this was right. He was innocent yet he had been unjustly condemned. He had lived his life under the laws of Athens and would not run away from them to save his life. He did not fear death at all. He was convinced that the soul survived death and, having lived a good life, had no terror of what lay beyond the grave. He died peacefully while his friends wept.

*

Socrates' story has much in common with that of Jesus. Both were good men; both were rejected by the leaders of their time; both renounced money, power, reputation and all the things that meant so much to so many people; both taught people to live good and unselfish lives; both men were unjustly tried and put to death; both could have escaped and both refused. Both men faced their death calmly and willingly and both believed in life after death.

Today, many would consider that Jesus and Socrates, as well as other great figures such as Plato, Aristotle, the Buddha, Mohammed or Gandhi, were all great men. They all taught us, in their different way, a great deal about how life should be lived. We can learn from all of them. They all rejected the norms of their society and showed, by their example and their teachings, that a different way of life was possible. In the West, the figure of Jesus has been the major model whilst in the East, the Buddha and Mohammed, as well as some of the Hindu religious leaders, have been more important and fulfil a similar role. All these men can, by their examples, help us to live better and more fulfilled lives.

Imagine that you were in Galilee in A.D. 30. A young, bearded prophet walks the hills. People flock to see him, yet the authorities disapprove. There are many self-proclaimed prophets throughout the known world at this time, just as there are many gods. The gods are considered to have some interest in the lives of men. Only one small group (the Israelites) consider that there is a single God – and their opinions are tolerated, even if they seem to most educated Greeks and Romans somewhat bizarre. The Roman Empire is tolerant of beliefs in local deities – religion is not, at this stage, a primary issue for the Empire and tolerance costs nothing. The young prophet has no money, no home, no worldly power, no influential friends. His message is simple and direct – yet others have had simple and direct messages. One of them, John, was recently imprisoned for expressing similar views. Who, then, is this prophet? John, from prison, sends messages to the man to ask the same question – 'Who are you?' The prophet does not reply directly. Instead he tells the messengers:

> Go back and tell John what you have seen and heard. The blind can see, the lame can walk, those who suffer from dreaded skin diseases are made clean, the deaf can hear, the dead are raised to life, and the good news is preached to the poor (Lk. 7:21–22).

In other words, John must make up his own mind. He must decide for himself. The situation for the man or woman in the twentieth century is no different from a contemporary of Jesus. True, his contemporaries could see Jesus and even touch him, but this really does not help in deciding who he is. Outwardly, there is nothing extraordinary. He is an ordinary man in almost every way. If we had a video of Jesus' life, this would not prove that he was other than a great teacher of moral truths – like Socrates.

Jesus' follower, Peter, was the first to acknowledge him. When pressed, he finally decided, 'this man is the son of

God'. It is this claim on which the whole Christian church is built. It is, however, a strange claim. How can a man be God? God is Almighty, Infinite, the Creator of all. A man is finite, limited and a created creature. To say that one individual is both God and man verges on the nonsensical. It is a claim that amounts to a paradox: yet this paradox is at the very heart of the Christian Church.

This claim that Jesus is both God and Man is the key factor that separates Jesus from Socrates. Socrates, Plato, Aristotle, the Buddha, Mohammed and Gandhi are all men – they never claimed to be anything else and nor did their followers claim any more about them. Only Christianity claims that God became man; that Jesus, the carpenter from Nazareth, was both fully man and fully God. Jesus is the absolute paradox.

To be sure, this paradox can be explained away. Jesus can be described as a man who was inspired by God or he can be looked on as God who only appears to be a man. Both positions have had their supporters over the last 2,000 years but both positions have been rejected. Neither position is true to the Christian claim – they are both heresies.

Socrates can, as a human being, bring us to see truths about ourselves and the way we live. He can show us new insights into the human condition. Socrates, however, as an individual, is not important – what is central is his message, the record that we have of his teachings and his approach to life. Jesus, however, is different.

If, as Christians claim, Jesus is God, then He is vitally important. He is not just another human being. Here we have God who has come down to be with us and to live as an ordinary man. He is not just another clever teacher. He is *the* Teacher. He can, as God, tell us and show us things that human reason cannot work out for itself: why we are here; what life is about; the choices available to us – and their consequences.

Within this world, human reason can discover many

things – truths about mathematics and science, astronomy, archeology, geology, geography, philately and philosophy. Truths about our everyday world can be discovered and can tell us more all the time about the Universe in which we live and how it is ordered. If our reason tries to comprehend God, however, what we end up doing is fitting God within our limited human categories and abolishing Him altogether. We no longer have an infinite and eternal creator God, we have a human construct. Only God himself, by undertaking, out of love, to become the Teacher, could bring us eternal truths, truth that goes beyond our human categories. Socrates cannot do this. He, like us, is limited to pushing back the horizons of our human knowledge, to seeking human truths – he can never go outside them.

Rationally, the claim that Jesus is both God and man, fully human and yet fully divine, does not appear to make sense. Reason has to be left behind and faith must take over. Reason cannot bring an individual to accept a paradox. Reason will always dismiss it or seek to reduce it to something that can be understood. If, therefore, philosophers or rational individuals examine the Christian claims, the temptation will always be to reinterpret these so as to reduce the Christian message to fit within the bounds of reason. Many, many seek to do this today – Don Cupitt's *Sea of Faith* series on BBC TV was a good example. David Jenkins, the Bishop of Durham, also adopts a rational approach. Philosophers such as Dewi Phillips (University of Cardiff), Professor Stewart Sutherland (now principal of King's College, London) and Maurice Wiles (Oxford) all affirm the priority of reason. There are few philosophers and theologians who will adopt a simple faith perspective in claims that go beyond reason – yet anything less is something other than Christianity.

When it comes to Christianity, the simple man knows as much as the wise man. The truly wise man comes to the conclusion that he, like Socrates, cannot understand certain things. The only difference between the simple man of faith and the wise man of faith is that the simple man understands nothing in rational terms and the wise man knows that he knows nothing. The dangerous stage is reached by the half-wise individual who thinks that he knows something, who writes books and articles in learned journals which show his cleverness and who substitutes a human construct for truth (as a philosopher of religion myself this charge strikes uncomfortably close to home!)

There are, of course, real difficulties with a too simple account that appeals to faith alone and leaves reason behind. The naïve appeal to non-rational belief may be dangerous and can be used by fanatics to breed division, misery and mayhem. The Christian is not saying, 'Believe in nonsense because it is nonsense and if we can think of half a dozen other nonsensical things before breakfast you had better believe in these too.' He or she is rather saying, 'Believe in the paradox of Jesus the God/Man because it is the only way that a God who really loves us as individuals could show that love. If you will only accept this, then the consequences of living the love relationship with God will become clear.'

Socrates and Jesus have a great deal in common. Both were very good men who taught a new way of living life, both lived and died by their beliefs in the sure conviction that they would survive death. The Christian claim, however, is that Jesus is God – it is this that makes Jesus unique. Socrates is only a man. The claim that Jesus is both fully God and fully man is a paradox and it goes beyond what reason can understand. It cannot be proved to be true and reason cannot get to grips with it.

If Christianity is based on a paradox, then in what sense can it claim to be true? This is our next problem.

3

And is it True?

He: *I believe there are more than 2000 billion stars. Why should God, if there is a God, bother about our little planet?*

She: *Do you know the story of the coal miner's daughter?*

The claim that the man, Jesus of Nazareth, is God: that he is both God and man, rests on paradox. Even if the claim that a man can be both finite and infinite at the same time made sense, why should God take on the figure of a relatively poor carpenter?

Imagine a young and beautiful coal miner's daughter living in a remote pit village in a Central European kingdom. Imagine further that the King had once seen this girl when he was out hunting and fell totally in love with her. He thought about her constantly and loved her passionately. He wished to woo her and to bring her to love him – yet how should he proceed? If he were to ride to the village with all his retainers, the girl would be terrified. If he stepped down and spoke to her in his magnificent clothes, she would quake with terror. If he said that he loved her, it simply would not make sense. She would be so full of fear, so awe-struck, so intimidated that she could not respond. Her fear might cause her to go along with whatever the King wished, but then she would not love him. The problem was that the King did not want to seduce her, to intimidate her or to make her his servant –

he loved her and he wanted her to love him. Nothing else would do.

If the King persists in his love, he really has only one alternative. Of course, his courtiers are likely to say that he is mad – why, after all, should the King bother with a poor, insignificant peasant girl? If he wanted her, he has but to command and she has no choice but to obey. If the King insists on giving her a choice, she is still certain to do as he wishes because she could not refuse him anything. The King sees, however, that the courtiers have misunderstood. They do not understand love. If the King truly loves the young girl, then he would never intimidate her or frighten her. He would not be interested in a relationship with her that is built on fear. Only one thing is good enough – and that is a relationship of love.

The King, therefore, has no alternative. He must go to the young girl in disguise. Not dressed in his fine robes, but rather in old clothes – the clothes of a wandering tradesman perhaps. He must hope that, when she sees him and gets to know him, she will fall in love with him. If she does, then the love will be free. She will love him for himself and not for any ulterior motive. She will not think of his money, of his power, of the comforts she could enjoy nor will she be full of fear of the consequences of not loving – she will love him for himself alone. There are, of course, risks. The young girl may not like the King. She may reject him and prefer another. This, however, is the risk that love runs. It can never be forced and it must risk rejection and disappointment.

The parallel, of course, is with God. If God appeared on earth as He is, everyone would be terror-struck. Instant obedience would be automatic. The Creator of the Universe disclosing Himself as He is would be more than man could cope with. The Jews recognised that no one could see God and live – He had to hide himself. If God came to earth in any obvious way, fear would reign and freedom would be lost. God, however, does not want this sort of response. It is easy (if you are God) to create obedient robots who will praise you and do as they have been programmed to do. Even if you are God, however, the most important and the most precious thing is something that you cannot create – it is the free response of love.

God may start by creating a world. This is full of beauty, and may give human beings freedom in the hope that men and women will learn of his goodness from the beauty around them. But they may choose to ignore this reality. They may refuse to recognise God's handiwork and may live their lives ignoring Him. Even if hints are sent (nothing can be too explicit as then freedom would be done away with) by prophets and wise men, these can easily be ignored. What, then, can God do? One alternative is to forget the whole enterprise – to abandon man: but love can never, ever, abandon the beloved, no matter what the beloved does.

God has only one alternative left – to come to earth himself, in the form of a man, to express as clearly as He is able what He is like, to tell people that God is love and wants nothing more and values nothing higher than a free response of love from each of us. God actually chooses, out of love, to suffer with man and to suffer for man – because only by God taking this step can man be brought to the possibility of the love relationship.

If our freedom is to be preserved, however, if we are to be able to respond in genuine love and without being forced, then God can only give this message indirectly. He must come to earth in the form of an ordinary human being – and He must risk the danger of people ignoring Him or rejecting His message. There simply is no other way forward. There is nothing further He can do.

God can come to earth as a man, He can live with very ordinary people loving and caring for the poor and despised in society – but He risks rejection. If He has to suffer a hideous and agonising death on the cross (and just how terrible a death crucifixion is, is sometimes forgotten amidst the plethora of Easter bunnies and eggs), this is a necessary price freely and willingly paid – out of love.

If we had been present with Jesus in Galilee then we might simply have seen a remarkable man. There was no proof that this was God. We would have had to come to recognise this for ourselves. We would have had to make a decision. It is easy for us to think, 'If we had only been present with Him, we would have recognised and followed him.' The chances are high that we would not. The crowd that shouted His praises on Palm Sunday were shouting for Him to be crucified a few days later. Everyone, even his closest friends, left Him. To acknowledge Jesus would have meant punishment and possibly death – Stephen, the first martyr, found this out soon after the resurrection. No, it was not a nice business being a friend of Jesus and most of us would have been far too frightened or far too attached to our comfortable and secure lives to acknowledge Him.

In the same way today, we can read the Bible, we can look at the history of the Christian Church and at people who call themselves Christians but we must make our own decision. If we decide to acknowledge Jesus and to follow Him we must recognise that the path will not be comfortable. It will be much easier and smoother to ignore His call and to turn away; much more pleasant not to think about the questions he asks us.

God is present everywhere in His creation, but never in any direct or obvious way. Always He communicates so as not to interfere with our freedom. God leaves us free to accept Him or not. There is no need for us to accept His message; it can be ignored or rejected. Even when Jesus says, 'He who has seen me, has seen the Father', we can easily dismiss this claim – we can refuse to take it seriously or just not think about it.

There is no division between Jesus the Son and God the Father. This is what the Christian teaching of the Trinity says. It sounds, of course, a tall order. For the poor travelling tradesmen to say to the young village girl, 'If you have seen me, you have seen the King' is implausible enough and she would be unlikely to believe him, but who is going to believe that a man can be God? Some signs can be given to His followers, to help them convince themselves and to help their lack of trust, but always the signs are ambiguous, always they can be interpreted away. Signs are never done where there is no faith – what is the point? Signs are meant to build faith and if there is no faith, there is nothing there to build. Signs alone cannot be a basis for faith – love is not based on 'magic tricks':

> 'How evil and godless are the people of this day!' Jesus exclaimed. 'You ask me for a miracle? No! The only miracle you will be given is the miracle of the prophet Jonah. In the same way that Jonah spent three nights in the big fish, so will the Son of Man spend three days in the depths of the earth (Matt. 12:39–40).

Pilate asked Jesus 'What is truth?' Pilate was seeking truth that was rational, that could be proved or demonstrated. He was seeking the sort of truth that philosophers like, truth grounded in certainty, where there are accepted methods of proof. The same question is asked today when people want proof of the truth of Christianity and of the existence of God. Many and various proofs have been put forward for the existence of God. None of them 'work' – if by 'work' is meant the demonstration of the existence of God or the truth of Christianity to a completely open-minded observer. If someone is already a believer or inclined towards belief, then the proofs may seem convincing – but alternative explanations are always available. A probability or 'cumulative case' approach can be taken by trying to argue that the existence of God is more likely than not but, again, the balance of probability is going to be largely dependent on our own ideas or pre-conceptions.

G.K. Chesterton said: 'You would sooner catch Leviathan on a hook than convert a soul on a syllogism.' Many books have been written trying to prove that God exists. The proofs are various – some start from facts in the world. The Design argument moves from particular features of the way the world is, to try to demonstrate a 'great designer'. Other arguments start from the existence of a contingent world – however far back we go in time, it is argued, we can never explain the world unless God exists. A God who necessarily exists and always has existed is a necessity if there is to be a universe at all. Yet other arguments seek to analyse the nature of God and to show why it is logical nonsense to deny God's existence. Another alternative is to start with the existence of morality or beauty in the world and to try to show that these features of man could not have evolved through natural selection – they have no survival value. God must, it is suggested, be responsible.

Much effort has been expended on these arguments, but they all depend on certain presuppositions and assumptions. If these are rejected, the arguments do not succeed. Believer and non-believer differ not so much on whether the arguments work but about the assumptions from which the arguments begin.

An awareness of God never starts from consideration of philosophic arguments. What is rather needed is an openness to God's presence; an openness to the beauty of creation and the wonder of man. We can either be 'open' or 'closed' as individuals. We can open ourselves to others and to God, or we can close ourselves down and retreat behind our outward façade. Only we can make this choice – first we need to make ourselves vulnerable. We need to open ourselves to other people and to recognise them as human beings. When I was in Southern Africa, one of the greetings of the rural Africans was 'I see you' – it is an acknowledgement that the visitor is recognised and accepted. In many of our dealings with others in the West, we never really 'see' the other person at all. All we see is their status, their function in life. We do not see them as individual human beings in any way. Similarly, few of us are really willing to open ourselves to God and to 'see' Him.

Too often in the modern world, individuals are treated as statistics, as numbers. Computers do not recognise individuals and their characteristics – they rather recognise numbers. They are not interested in our names but in our number – our identity comes from a numerical reference. Our humanity can be thereby diminished.

The media talks of the unemployment figures – we are told that about two and a half million people are out of work in Britain. This is horrifying enough, but the figure does not take account of the misery of many of these individual human beings. Behind the statistic are fathers who have been out of work for months or even years, who cannot afford to buy Christmas presents for their children, who have no goal or purpose in life and who lounge around the house having spent months applying for jobs and being rejected. Behind the figures lie young people who have left school with no hope of a job – who see a future of unemployment stretching before them. Behind the figures are married women whose children are at school and who want to work, but cannot find any firm interested in what they have to offer. The figures enable us to be horrified by the problem in abstract, but to avoid facing up to the human misery behind the statistics.

The best testimony I have ever seen to the existence of God is the many people who have found Him. These are not bigoted individuals, not brain-washed individuals, not old people frightened of death and taking refuge in religion. They are well-balanced, normal and intelligent people who have staked their lives on God's presence in their lives or simple rural people who live their lives constantly aware of God's presence with them – their simple faith contrasting well with the sophistication of the philosophers and their arguments. They have been willing to open themselves to God and, by so doing, to let Him into their lives.

The foolishness of Pilate's question is precisely that it is addressed to Jesus. The Christian claim is that Jesus was God: that Jesus is the truth. Jesus says, 'I am the way, the truth and the life'. To ask 'What is truth?' when standing before the man who is the truth shows the confusion. The truth that Jesus is God cannot be proved. There is simply no way that Jesus could have 'proved' to Pilate that He was God – except by such a demonstration of power that would have, inevitably, destroyed human freedom. Calling down 'legions of angels' as He was challenged to do would have destroyed the very possibility that God became man to maintain – the possibility of a free response, in love, by each of us. Jesus had to remain fully man with his true identity hidden. If Pilate could not see that Jesus was God, nothing more could be said. Jesus' position must remain ambiguous – to be seen by faith and in love, but not by means of rational enquiry.

Pilate was doing his job. As an individual, he would have liked to dismiss the charges against Jesus, but he was warned by the Jewish leaders of the consequences of doing this. He had a duty to Caesar and his position depended on him doing his duty. He therefore put the presence of Jesus aside and stuck to the political realities – these dictated crucifixion. At least he was honest enough with himself to realise what he was doing – he solemnly washed his hands of Jesus' death. This symbolic gesture was not, however, effective. He was an individual and he had to take responsibility for his action. His refusal to be 'open' and his decision to hide behind his official position was something with which he would have to live, and die.

If someone asks me to prove to them that Mozart's music is beautiful, then I may try to show them this beauty. I may talk about the people who have been profoundly influenced by Mozart, I may take the person to concerts where particularly beautiful pieces by Mozart are played,

I may get musicians to discuss Mozart and the effect his music has on them. If, in spite of this, the person says, 'Yes, I can see that some think that Mozart is beautiful. I do not share that view and I think it is just a matter of personal opinion' then, at the end of the day, there is nothing more that I can say. The person must, indeed, make his or her own decision. No 'proof' is available.

If, to take another example, someone enjoys inflicting pain on others, then I cannot prove to him that this is wrong. I may show the consequences of his actions, I may warn of prison sentences, I may set out the dangers to society and the pain and hurt that is being inflicted but if, at the end of the day, the person says, 'Well, I appreciate that I must not get caught, because then I will be put in prison, but I really cannot see that it is wrong', then there is nothing more I can say. The obvious answer in this case is to call for the psychiatrist because we say that there is something wrong with a person who does not respond as we do. We do not take the same view with someone who cannot see beauty – or the truth that Jesus is God. The difference, of course, is that the latter cases do not harm anyone but themselves.

Love cannot be forced, nor can it be proved. Love demands a free response and is always vulnerable. The person who loves another may be willing to stake his or her whole life on this love, but they cannot 'prove' the love in a rational sense. I love my wife, but cannot prove why. If I try to describe my wife, Anne, it does not show why I love her. I may say that she is 5' 7" tall, has mouse-coloured hair, the first tiny middle-aged wrinkles, child-bearing hips and a reasonable I.Q. No such description, however, can begin to capture why I love her. What I love goes beyond any description.

The demand for a proof for Christianity rests on a misunderstanding of the God/man. You cannot prove a paradox to be true. Reason cannot go beyond itself and, if reason is in the driving seat, then the paradox is absurd. If reason

tells us that a man cannot also be Almighty God, that the
Creator cannot also be a created creature, then it is hardly
possible to rely on reason to bring us to see that Jesus is
God.

Love is higher than reason. It goes beyond reason. We
are complete human beings. We have minds that we can
use to calculate and to work things out for ourselves, but
we are far more than computers. We can respond with our
emotions, we can appreciate beauty, we have a moral sense,
we can be unselfish and be willing to put our own interests
in second place to those around us. None of these essential
parts of our humanity are 'intellectual'. We respond to
people and to the decisions about our lives as whole individuals. Philosophers and 'clever thinkers' seldom recognise this. They do away with almost everything that is
human about us except for our intellect. If they then
demand that the intellect prove the truth of Christianity
then, of course, it is impossible.

Anyone who thinks, however, that we are just intellectual
machines has a poor view of humanity.

Two responses are possible to the claim that Jesus is both
God and man. Reason may take offence at the paradox and
reject it – thus the person who thinks of herself as purely
intellectual will simply not accept the idea that Jesus can
be both God and Man. Since reason cannot understand
the paradox, since it offends against reason, the intellectual
person will reject it. Jesus was quite realistic in recognising
this possibility, thus he says, 'Blessed are they who are not
offended in me'. St. Paul proclaims that he preaches 'Christ
crucified – to the Jews a stumbling block and to the Greeks
folly'. To the Greeks (and, in the ancient world, the Greeks
were considered as the philosophers), the claim that a man
is God is folly – it is stupid, it is irrational. Even the Jews
regarded the incarnation as a stumbling block. God, they
considered, was unknowable and unnameable, beyond
human comprehension. To say that an individual man was
the Christ amounted to blasphemy.

The alternative response is faith – the acceptance that it is true that Jesus was God, even though this truth cannot be proved. The person who is content to remain committed to God, in faith and trust, even when this faith calls him or her beyond reason, will have nothing to hold onto but God alone. Reason has been left behind and cannot help.

At the end of the day, when faith confronts faith or when world-outlook confronts world-outlook, the truth of Christianity rests on an ultimate value judgement that cannot be further justified: the judgement that Jesus is God. Socrates, as a human being like us, was faced with a similar problem when deciding how to live his life and what would be the grounding of this life. He said, 'I cannot prove the immortality of the soul, but I am ready to stake my whole life on this "if".'

The Christian's position is similar. He or she cannot prove that Jesus is God and that it is possible to love God with 'All one's heart and mind and strength'. Each of us *can*, however (and, as we shall see, *should* if the Christian claim is genuine), be willing to stake our whole life on this 'if'. The possibility of being deluded must always remain open – even the saints experienced 'dark nights of the soul' in which God felt very far away indeed. The further the relationship with God develops, however, the less doubt there will be. It is a bit like swimming. It is only by swimming (not by reading about it) that we can learn to swim at all and thereby understand what swimming is like. Similarly, it is only the person who has set out to seek God who will be able to understand what the peace and love of God means.

God's grace, his willingness to enter into a love relationship, is available to everyone – but some response is required. Whenever He is sought, He will be found. Jesus himself said 'Seek and you shall find, knock and it shall be opened unto you'. If you really want to swim, you can – but first you must take a decision to be willing to get wet! You will not find God by reading this or any other book –

He will be found only in prayer and when we turn our lives wholeheartedly towards Him.

Mathematical, scientific and historical facts can be proved to be true. They rest on claims to truth that are validated by reason. The truth of Christianity is different. Because God came to earth out of love for man in the hope of bringing individuals into a personal love relationship with Him, God has to leave man free to respond. Love cannot be forced. Each of us must, therefore, decide on the truth of the Christian claim. Each of us must answer the question for ourselves: 'Who was this man?' Each of us can turn towards God or away from Him.

Pilate placed the emphasis on the wrong way of looking at truth. He sought facts that could be verified and was, therefore, offended by Jesus' failure to produce such facts. Pilate looked on truth in the same way as a philosopher looks on it. The truth that Jesus is God can, however, only be seen by each of us on an individual basis. We need to make a decision – for or against.

4

A New Way of Seeing?

He: *If Christianity cannot be proved to be true, then all you are saying is that it suits you, it is true for you. Fair enough – but not for me!*

She: *Truth does not depend on personal opinion. Jesus either was God, or he was not.*

The claim that Jesus is fully a man and fully God at the same time cannot be proved to be true in the way that scientific claims can be proved. The University of London has one college (Heythrop) which specialises entirely in theology and philosophy. It has a history stretching back over 350 years, although it has only been part of London University since 1971. Its library has more than 250,000 books – some of them dating back to the fifteenth century. All this accumulated learning combined in one of the finest theological libraries in Britain cannot prove that the absolute paradox of Jesus being both God and man is true. This claim goes beyond reason, and no matter how clever philosophers and theologians may be, they cannot prove something to be true that goes beyond reason.

It is either true or false that Caesar had an apple for breakfast on the morning that he landed in Britain. Perhaps we can never prove this to be true or false, but the truth or falsity of the claim that Caesar did eat an apple does not depend on whether or not we can prove its truth now or at any time in the future. Similarly, it is either true or false that the man, Jesus of Nazareth, was also God.

Even if one could prove that God existed, this would not prove the truth of Christianity. It is logically possible that God exists and yet Jesus was no more than a prophet (as the Muslims claim) or even an ordinary but misguided man. Even if people say that they believe that God exists, most do not take the further step of believing in God, of trusting their lives to Him.

Christianity calls each of us to believe and trust in God, a belief and trust based on love. This is not simply a matter of intellectual assent, nor is it a matter of people gathering in a church and saying certain things on Sunday. It is a matter of the truth of Christianity becoming 'true for you', as an individual. Only when Christianity becomes 'true for you' so that you are willing to stake your whole life on it, does it really become true in your own case.

Some existentialist philosophers, such as Sartre, have said that the important thing for each of us is to decide on our own truth and then to live by it. Whatever we live by is then true for us. The important thing is to live an authentic human existence and any life dedicated to a particular truth is authentic. The Christian position is not the same as this. The Christian claim is a realist claim – it is the claim that it is factually true that a creator God exists who loves each individual and that God became man in Jesus, died on the cross and rose from the dead. But it is not enough just to accept the truth of this by, for instance, reciting the Creed in a Church. As St James' epistle says, 'You believe in God? You do well. The devils also believe, and tremble.'

Belief that God exists does not come near to what Christianity is about. It is only when the factual truth of Christianity becomes 'true for us' so that it becomes the centre of our lives around which our whole existence revolves that we, as individuals, can see what Christianity involves.

At my college, some of the students organised a meeting and invited five members of staff to answer questions. One of the questions was this: 'Is it necessary for a Christian to assent to the dual nature of Christ?' My reply was that I thought that most ordinary people would not even understand what the question meant. If only those people who assented to this could be Christians, then Christianity was becoming an intellectual business. In fact, the question is quite straightforward – it is really asking if one has to believe that Jesus was both man and God. For anyone to think that this sort of question is what is central in Christianity seems to me to largely miss the point.

Two people may both say they believe in God, they may both go to Church and say the Creed, they may both be pillars of society, they may, in other words, be outwardly very similar indeed. One, however, may have actually realised the truth of Christianity and the consequences this will have for him or her, whilst for the other Christianity remains at an external level and has not been taken on board. In the case of the first individual, the 'penny has dropped', in the case of the second it has not.

Imagine a page consisting of some light and heavily shaded areas. What can be seen? Some people may say 'All I see are some differently shaded areas'. Another may say 'I see the head of a bearded man'. One of my colleagues had this illustration by his bedside for several months. Friends told him that it was a picture of a bearded man – but he could not 'see it'. One night, he got up, put on his bedside light, glanced at the picture – and there was the bearded man. It was quite obvious and he could not imagine how he had not seen it before. Once he had seen it, he could never understand how he could have been so blind. Take another example. It was drawn by the philosopher Wittgenstein. What does it represent? There are, in fact, two alternatives – it could be either a duck or a rabbit. Once you have 'seen' that both are possibilities, it will be obvious. But it may not be so obvious at first.

The 'duck-rabbit' example is, in fact, not an ideal one when related to the truth of the absolute paradox of the God/Man, Jesus Christ. Whether the drawing is of a duck or a rabbit, or both, depends on how it is seen. The claim that Christianity is true, however, does not depend on whether or not believers see things in a certain way. The Christian claim is that it is true that Jesus was fully God and fully man, but each individual must be brought, subjectively, to see this truth for him or herself.

Coming to see the truth of Christianity does not involve just accepting factual belief claims. It does not mean just saying the Christian creed – although it may start here. It means each of us coming to understand what it is for Christianity to become 'true for me', what Christianity is going to involve when it is taken on board and lived. Once we see and understand this, we then each of us have to decide whether or not we wish to try to live it – but that is our free choice. Until we have understood what is involved, however, we cannot even make the decision.

Christianity requires passion and total commitment – a commitment to a lived love relationship with God. The relationship has practical consequences and these can, to an extent, be foreseen. One of the purposes of this book is to examine what these consequences are for each one of us.

If Christianity requires each of us to see the truth for ourselves, how can Christianity be communicated? 'Jesus saves' notices, car stickers, large posters outside churches and the like will really not help a great deal. If Christianity centred around factual truths, then what would be needed would be erudite books by learned theologians which would explain these truths. Just as a teacher passes on facts to children in a history or geography lesson, so the Christian would seek to teach people facts – facts, perhaps, about Jesus' life or the teaching of the church. If they were Evangelicals, the 'facts' might revolve round the Bible, if they were Catholics, the 'facts' might centre on the meaning and understanding of the sacraments. Concentration on facts, however, will not bring anyone to see the subjective truth of Christianity – it will not bring us to the point at which we see that Christianity is true for us and how it must affect all our life.

If the paradox that Jesus was both God and Man is true, then its truth needs to be recognised by each of us on an individual basis. It is not a matter of a crowd of people agreeing to a series of propositions. It is a matter of each of us coming, for ourselves, to accept the fact that Jesus was God. It is not a matter of outward observance of a series of rules or agreeing to a particular creedal formulation.

Many churches and the priests within them concentrate on rules and creeds. It is easier to control people by ensuring they behave in a certain way or to get young people to learn facts rather than bringing them to understand what a relationship with God involves. Most religious education concentrates on the externals such as religious festivals and beliefs. In so doing, it misses the main point of Christianity.

There are parallels with sex education in schools. Most schools teach the facts about sex education and teach them well. There are diagrams and models and by the time their education is complete, boys and girls know how to do what with which and which becomes what in certain circumstances. Their factual knowledge is accurate. Schools too often ignore the much more important area, however – how to bring young people to understand about love and what love involves. This is a much more important topic, but it is also very difficult to teach. You cannot teach facts about love – you need to bring someone to see for themselves what a relationship of love is. You need to communicate with them not directly (which would involve facts) but indirectly. You need to bring them to 'see for themselves' the importance of love. This is probably better shown by personal example or discussion on a one-to-one basis than in a classroom situation.

The emphasis is constantly put on the wrong way of looking at central questions in life. Consider the following:

1) What does it mean to love someone?

2) What does it mean to get married?

3) What does it mean to pray?

4) What does it mean to be a Christian?

5) What does it mean to die?

These questions can be answered in two ways – factually or from our own point of view. The factual approach concentrates on the objective meaning of the question. For instance to get married involves making certain promises in a church or register office, it requires ceremonies and social practices which have grown up round them, it involves certain expectations about children and future conduct and it has tax and financial implications. Similarly in the case of death, there are many factual issues involved. Death is defined by doctors in a certain way dependent on lack of brain activity, it has financial and legal consequences which will affect relatives and perhaps friends of the one who dies, the body has to be disposed of, various legal formalities have to be gone through including the issue of a death certificate and perhaps, in certain circumstances, a *post mortem* examination. Again these factors all approach the question of death from a factual point of view and, whilst interesting, are not the most important way of looking at the questions.

The decisive way of approaching all the above questions is to consider their effects on us, as individuals. Take the questions 'What does it mean for me if I love someone?',

'What does it mean for me to get married?' and 'What does it mean for me to die?' These ask us about how we are related to the questions and they can only be answered by each of us, subjectively and individually. They become questions for you and I and the easy factual answers are not very helpful. The questions ask us about the meaning of love, marriage and death and how our lives will be affected by these.

The same applies to the question of 'What does it mean to be a Christian?' Factually this question asks about beliefs, external behaviour, church membership, feasts and festivals. The important way of looking at the question, however, is to see it as asking each of us, 'What does it mean *for me* to be a Christian?' This is much more uncomfortable and challenging. There is no single 'right' answer – each of us needs to think the answer through for ourselves.

Many churches concentrate on facts and rituals and ignore the subjective elements. Two young friends of mine, Leah and Catherine, were given a Catholic diary by their convent school. On the back page is a section headed 'Duties of Catholics today'. The first three and sixth duties are as follows:

1) To keep holy the day of the Lord's resurrection; to worship God by participating in Mass every Sunday and holy day of obligation; to avoid those activities which would hinder renewal of soul and body, e.g. needless work and business activities, unnecessary shopping, etc.,

2) To lead a sacramental life; To receive Holy Communion frequently and the sacrament of penance regularly. The minimum is fulfilment of the Easter obligation,

3) To study Catholic teaching at all times but especially in preparation for the sacrament of confirmation, to be

confirmed and then to continue to study and advance
Christ's cause,

6) To do penance including abstaining from meat and
fasting from food on the appointed days, and observing
Friday as a day of special penance.

It is interesting the extent to which the above sees Catholicism as resting on 'duties'. The duties are almost all
external – the Catholic must go to Mass, avoid certain
activities, take Holy Communion and the sacrament of
penance, study Church teachings, abstain from meat and
fast on certain days. They all look on religion in external
terms – they are objective rules which can be clearly laid
down and whose observance can be monitored externally.
There is no mention here of love, no reference to a lived
love relationship with God leading to love of neighbour.
The emphasis has been shifted from a lived life of love to
external observances.

I am, in fact, far from sure that the above is a true
reflection of Catholicism today – but it is an impression
that many people are still given and which many of the
older generation in the Church still accept. The idea of
Christianity resting on a lived love relationship is still a
minority view.

It is certainly not only the Catholic Church which
concentrates on externals. The Church of England is
constantly concerned with finance and committee work,
many services are primarily social affairs and the extent of
real commitment is sometimes far too small. The Evangelical Churches are in many ways similar. Again, the
concentration can be on the externals; on the emotions, on
hymn-singing and the creation of feelings of near-euphoria
which can be generated by communal praise. The accent
tends to be on the communal by itself with little of the
loneliness and the uncertainty of the individual in a lived
love relationship with God. There can also be a real fear

of silence and of being alone with God as well as a fear of questioning beliefs or using reason to study theological or philosophical questions.

Membership of a church can certainly give a feeling of belonging, of being part of a community, and this is good and right. But there are dangers. There can be a danger in a feeling of belonging to one group as this can foster the illusion that 'our group is right' and other groups are either wrong or, at least, less right than we are. This is but a short step from intolerance.

Just possibly, when we die and come into the presence of the living God, what will matter is not what Church label we have worn but whether, with passion and dedication, we try to follow the Christian path. Some cemeteries still have separate areas for Anglicans, Baptists, Catholics and Methodists – as though it is our denominational label that is important. Seen from God's point of view this must, surely, be childishness.

Jesus prayed that all his followers should be one – possibly the unity we need to share is not that of a single building or a single form of worship, but rather a single commitment, a single vision and a single dedication. If these were one, the denominational barriers would cease to matter.

The attraction of putting the emphasis on facts and outward rituals is that they can be easily communicated. Priests and church leaders can 'talk at' their congregations without the need for the much more difficult process of bringing the individual to think for him or herself. If, however, each of us, as individuals, are given priority, then a different form of communication is required.

Indirect communication is the process by which each of us can be brought to see truth for ourselves. Each of us must come to decide on the truth of Christianity for ourselves. Instead of having people 'talk at' us, each of us needs to be brought to the point at which we can see for ourselves what Christianity involves. There is, of course, no guarantee that any of us will see this – we may be too busy, too disinterested, too preoccupied with our own concerns to open ourselves to the possibility of a new outlook on life – particularly one that may challenge our comfortable way of living.

Even if we come to see what Christianity involves, even if we accept that it is factually true, we may not be willing to take it on board and to live by it. All that each of us can do for another is to bring him or her to the moment of decision, to the point at which the person we are relating to can see what Christianity involves and can then make a personal decision. No one can do more.

The most that one of us can do for another is to act as a midwife to faith. When a woman is having a baby, the woman and baby are the individuals who are important. The midwife will be there to encourage and advise or, possibly, to give a pull and push at decisive moments. After the birth, the midwife is often forgotten and many women will not even know the name of the midwife who helped them. So it should be with faith – one of us can help another towards a relationship with God, but we must never get in the way.

The best way for a Christian to communicate his or her faith is to try to live it, to show the love that Christianity should involve in every aspect of life. This will make more impression and be a more effective witness to the truth of Christianity than any number of learned lectures. What is more, it is something that each of us can do, in whatever walk of life we may be. The only requirement is for us *really* to take Christianity seriously. Very few people actually do this. They pay lip service to Christ, but do not allow Him to affect their lives. As Jesus warned, we need to beware of people who are 'wolves in sheep's clothing'. Most of all, we need to ask ourselves whether we are the wolf whom few people recognise under the sheep-like exterior that we put on!

I was coming down the stairs at my college one day and

greeted a middle-aged student whom I had not seen for
about a year. Cheerfully I asked how he was. He looked
at me seriously and replied, 'I've never been the same since
that comment you made to me on the stairs'. He would
not tell me what it was and I went away appalled. More
than a year before, I must have said something, in passing,
and had given no more thought to it – yet this remark had
hurt someone and had had an affect which had lasted all
that time. I sometimes wonder if part of being in hell might
be going over all the times when one has hurt someone or
has affected someone without even knowing it. This would
apply even more if indirect communication is taken seriously. It is in our lives that we can most clearly show the
truth of Christianity, yet our lives all too rarely do this.
We may turn many people away from Christ just by the
way we act.

The danger of some modern, high-profile religious
leaders is that a person can be led to focus attention on
them rather than on God. Alternatively, if one person
believes because of their admiration for another then when
that other turns out to have feet of clay (as so many of us
do), faith will be undermined. The truth of Christianity
must be accepted for itself alone, and not because we are
relying on someone else.

Socrates saw himself as a midwife and, among humans,
this is the highest possibility. He was grateful for his
'favourable' appearance. It was favourable because he was
not at all attractive – he even had growths on his face. He
felt glad that, because of this, people would not listen to
him because of his appearance but because, in listening to
the questions he raised, they began to understand things
for themselves.

Christianity is a religion of freedom and of love and love
does not judge. One person may have become aware of the
possibility of living the love relationship with God and may
try to bring someone else to see that this is the most
important thing in the world – but they cannot prove it,

nor can they force the other into the relationship. Each individual must make up his or her own mind and their decision must be respected.

Indirect communication is not coercive. It respects the freedom of the other and does not look for results. One of us may never know the effect of what he or she has said or done on another and, in a way, we should not be concerned with results. The most each of us can do is to try to communicate the truth to someone else – and this may well best be done by silence and by just 'being'; by letting our actions and conduct speak for themselves. This is a quiet and unassertive way of bringing people to the truth, but it may well be the only really effective way.

The modern world is preoccupied with facts and each of us, as individuals, appears to be increasingly unimportant and insignificant. We seem to be like cogs in some vast machine.

Christianity is not a matter of learning facts (although it is obviously necessary to know the basic essentials). It rather involves 'Belief in God' (meaning trust and commitment) rather than 'Belief that God exists'. Each of us needs to come to accept that God became a man out of love for us, that He loves us tremendously and that we are really important to Him. This needs to become 'true for us'. We cannot be brought to love someone by being taught facts. We can only enter into a love relationship on our own.

The most one person can do for another is to act as a midwife to faith – helping us to understand what a relationship with God which affects the whole of life actually means. There we must be left, alone, to make our own decisions.

5

'Loving' and Being 'in Love'

He: *I am happy enough in the life I am living. I do not see much alternative and do not see what difference God makes. I have quite a few friends; what more can I expect?*

She: *You have not mentioned love. I love you as well as my mother – but I do not think I am* in *love with either of you.*

Love is an over-used and under-analysed word. It is used constantly in romantic stories, in the media and in religious books, yet its meaning is far from clear and seems to shift all the time.

What is the difference between 'loving' someone and being 'in love'? If we are 'in love' with someone, that person is the centre of our life. The obvious example is when a young man or woman are 'in love'. For them, life centres on the beloved. They wait for every telephone call or the next letter. Days are spent looking forward to the evening or the weekend when they will next meet.

Because being 'in love' places another person at the centre of our life, we cannot be in love with more than one person at a time – our lives cannot have more than one centre. By contrast, we can certainly love more than one person. But it is not only people with whom we can fall in love. Sometimes we centre our lives on our hobbies (football, chess, television, birds, stamp collecting, beer, the

Women's Institute or the like) or on our job. Many of us centre our whole lives on our career – we are, in effect, 'in love' with our job.

By definition, if we place a hobby or our job at the centre of our life, everything else will take second place. If it comes to a choice, the hobby or our work comes first. Imagine that you have a friend whom you really care for and he contacts you and needs your help. You have a stamp exhibition coming up (or whatever else may be your central hobby) which you want to attend. Which takes first place, your friend or your hobby? The same question can be asked about your career – is your job more important than people? Do you treat people as individuals who matter or does your job take over so that you become like an 'official robot', cold and indifferent to everything but form filling?

Each of us needs to make a decision about the centre of our life. What has absolute priority for us? Most people never really think about this question, but it is vital.

We allow our lives to drift from one thing to another with little thought. We leave school or university and the job we go into may owe more to chance than to careful thought. After a few years, again by chance, we may meet someone to whom we feel attracted and become engaged and get married. For a short time, the other person is the centre of our life – we are 'in love'. A house is now needed and also a mortgage. Furniture must be purchased and success in the job is now essential if financial obligations are to be met. A few years later, perhaps, the first baby arrives. Soon the house is too small and, in any case, greater success at work deserves a larger house. This, in turn, means a bigger mortgage. So our lives continue. Our marriages may or may not be happy, but the car and the status that goes with it become important to us. We need a bigger colour television, a video, home computer and, perhaps, a small sailing boat and holiday abroad: these are now all considered necessities. So life goes on – rarely planned by us – and we react to events as they happen rather than shaping them. Our lives have no clear centre and we have little long-term purpose.

Most people's lives are fairly empty and, therefore, need distractions. Often these are found in spending money. Almost every morning the post brings letters which tell me of things that I 'need'. In fact, I do not need them at all, but if my life is not full and does not have a focus I can easily come to think that by spending money the vacant space will be filled. We experience the gap, buy some of the advertised products (which, curiously, do not seem to fill the gap) and so life continues. It is all pleasant enough but, just occasionally, we may begin to wonder what it is all about.

Socrates said, 'The unexamined life is not worth living,' whilst Apollo's watchword was, 'know yourselves'. Most of us do not examine our lives or ourselves or, if we do, we do not follow our thinking through. Since no one else seems to address these questions, they can easily be regarded as unimportant. The shortest horror story in the world is this:

> *What happens to women who marry dull men?*
> *They go into the suburbs, and never come out again.*

The horror of this is not the suburbs – there is nothing wrong with suburbs, town or country. It is the frightening prospect of the young woman who falls in love, marries without too much reflection and suddenly finds that her life is a vacuum – with little centre or meaning other than her 'dull' husband. In fact, the husband may not be particularly dull, it is just that he has never thought for himself; he has never considered the alternatives. He has never considered the meaning of his life or how his wife can be allowed to be an individual and to develop her own talents. In spite of the rise in the feminist movement, there are still many, many women who end up trapped by their duty to their children and with little real chance for self-development.

Men and women are free. We have the ability to make choices in our lives and they can be *our* choices – not those of our friends, parents or our peer group. We can be free individuals. Not everyone agrees with this – as an example, the following limerick by Maurice Hare does not:

> *There once was a man who said; 'Damn!*
> *It is born in upon me I am,*
> *An engine that moves,*
> *In pedestrian grooves,*
> *I'm not even a bus, I'm a tram'.*

A tram has to keep to the tram lines. It has no choice on the direction it takes. So, some people have held, we are not free – we are like trams and have no choice but to follow the tram lines laid out by our genes and our background. This view Christianity rejects. We are free, we can choose. If, however, each of us is to make a choice about our life, we need to be clear on the alternatives. One of the best ways of approaching this is to ask who or what lies at the centre of our existence or, to put it another way:

1) What or who are we in love with at the present time? and

2) What or who would we like to be in love with?

1) and 2) are often not the same!

If these questions are taken seriously, what are the alternatives? There are five possibilities:

i) The unreflective life
If my life does not have a centre then it will be dominated by external events. In a way, this is not the life of an

individual at all, although it is the life that most of us lead. We do not direct our life to any particular end and we are not in control of our destiny. We are like a ship, out of control in the middle of a storm, blown this way and that by external forces without any attempt or effort to head in a certain direction. All the captain can do is to react to events; he does not plot a course or have a plan. This is an all too common possibility, but it is unlikely to be one that many of us would choose.

When students meet together at university or college they may well discuss questions such as 'What is life about?' or 'Does our existence have any meaning?' These issues are debated long and hard – sometimes far into the night. They are issues that matter and should be central for us. Although it is enjoyable to discuss them, however, we rarely take any decision and, having talked about them, just let events take over so that we drift where circumstances and outside forces take us.

ii) *The life of pleasure*

Each of us is different and we find our pleasures in different activities. Some of us pursue particular hobbies; others seek power, fame, reputation, success or money; others seek a quiet family life; yet others find their pleasure in helping people ('She lived for others. You can tell the others by their hunted look!'); whilst some turn to drink, drugs or sex. Whatever the activity, however, the aim of this sort of life is the same – the maximisation of pleasure and the minimising of pain.

If we decide to base our lives on enjoying ourselves as much as possible, we need to think through how to maximise our pleasure. Take the case of someone whose passion and interest lies in fishing. At first sight, one might think that his pleasure comes from catching fish, but this is not the case. If it was, the best way to achieve the objective would be to throw a grenade into the river. All the fish in the area of the grenade would be killed and the fisherman could pick them up further downstream. But a fisherman would be horrified at such a thought. The real pleasure is in the chase – many fishermen actually throw their fish back when they have been caught whilst the real purists will fish only with a dry fly, as this is the most skilled and difficult way to catch fish.

One of the weaknesses with this sort of life is that it is vulnerable to events which are beyond our control. So many things are outside our control. Imagine a person who seeks political power. She may, with many years of dedicated work, get elected to parliament – only to find that sitting on the backbenches gives almost no power at all. She therefore struggles onwards, again seeking further power, and may even get a junior ministerial appointment. Suddenly some event may happen which is beyond her control. She may have a road accident or a heart attack; her party may lose an election; she may make a mistake which costs her her job; a new Prime Minister may come to power who no longer views her with favour. All at once, everything on which she has built her life lies in ruins.

Tolstoy, in a marvellous short story called *The Death of Ivan Illyich*, tells of a young man who qualifies as a lawyer and sets out to seek success. Ivan works hard, makes the most of his chances and is promoted. He marries reasonably well and the newly married couple buy a house in a good neighbourhood where many similar professional people live. They have two children and the husband is eventually appointed to be a judge. They move to a larger house and take pleasure in furnishing it tastefully – although in fact it is furnished in a very similar way to all the other houses of their professional friends.

Ivan's life is successful, his wife has two children and family life settles down into a routine. He is very busy and is promoted to be a judge. Then, when he is in his early sixties, he develops cancer. The doctors make non-committal noises and put him on various drugs. Some seem to work, others do not. Gradually Ivan slips further down hill and the pain increases. He takes three months to die and in this period his wife and two daughters, although they do their duty, really begin to consider him a nuisance. His wife is preoccupied with the pension she will get when he dies. The daughters have their own busy lives to live and visit him out of obligation. The only one who genuinely cares is his servant, Gerasim. Ivan lies in bed, dying, and looks back over his life. Finally he is brought to ask himself the dreaded question as to whether, perhaps, the whole of his life is based on a mistake. It is only in his last few moments that he can actually face up to this fact. It is in dying that he first becomes an individual and he realises, too late, the wasted life he has led.

Here is an example of a life devoted to pleasure – although not in any clearly focused sense. Pleasure is sought in worldly success and reputation and in the good opinion of friends and colleagues. Such a life may, indeed, be very enjoyable, but circumstances may well lead the person (as it did Ivan) to see that it is empty. By the time one of us realises this, it may be too late to turn back. The options have been narrowed to such an extent and habits have become so deeply ingrained that there are no longer real alternatives. In all too many cases this leads to depression and despair. The life devoted to pleasure:

1) Is vulnerable to circumstances which we cannot control and which lie outside ourselves, and

2) Is likely, in the end, to disappoint and to lead us to feel that our life has been wasted.

In spite of this, we need to recognise that this appears to be an attractive option. Who, after all, would not like to have as much pleasure as possible and to be free from pain? Partly, of course, we need to consider where real pleasure lies. If we choose this option, we must ask ourselves whether the things that appear so pleasant to us in the short term are really likely to provide long term satisfaction. As we lie on our.deathbed, will we be able to look back over our lives and to feel it has been well spent?

iii) The moral life

Socrates tried to show the people of Athens that all the normal ends that they sought were misplaced. Instead of chasing after worldly preoccupations, we should seek to become virtuous and good individuals. We should not allow our lives to be dominated by seeking external results – the aim should rather be to seek mastery of the self so that we are 'in control of the house of our bodies'. We should seek to do 'the good' in every situation, without compromise and without fear of the consequences.

Few people are really prepared to act on principle without thinking in terms of the results. Most individuals will adopt almost any means which will achieve the results they want. T.S. Eliot in his poem *The Rock* put it this way:

> *All men are ready to invest their money*
> *But most expect dividends.*
> *I say to you: make perfect your will.*
> *I say, take no thought of the harvest,*
> *But only of proper sowing.*

In other words, the person who is trying to live the moral life for itself alone will seek to act morally in every circumstance without regard to the consequences. A friend of mine provided a good example of this sort of life. He was a young, burly garage mechanic – good at his job; thorough and methodical. He worked for a large Ford dealer in south-east England, but he was continually getting into difficulties. The garage laid down set times for various servicing jobs that all the mechanics had to achieve. They were paid on the basis of these set times. Say, for instance, that on a particular car a set time of two hours was allowed to take out the wheel bearings, to clean them and re-pack with new grease. My friend found that, to really do the job properly, it would take him three hours. Partly this was because he was not a fast worker; partly it was because he was very thorough. A number of his fellow mechanics had similar difficulties, but they would take short cuts. Sometimes they would not bother to take the bearings out and clean them – they would just pack in a bit of extra grease, leaving the old grease in place. This, obviously, was much quicker than doing the job properly and no one would know once the wheel assembly was put back.

My friend, however, would have none of this. He insisted on doing every job thoroughly. The result was that he was by far the slowest mechanic in the workshop and was eventually dismissed. He simply was not prepared to compromise – he would do his job well, whatever the consequences.

Most of us compromise all the time in our lives but the person living the moral life will not do so. This is very different from the pleasure-seeking life set out above. Often the demands of morality will be painful and unpleasant and will give the very opposite of pleasure. They may involve sacrifice and suffering. My friend was putting his financial and job interests in second place to what he believed to be right – he would not take the easy way out.

If any of us centre our life on morality, we will never lie, steal, commit adultery or contravene the moral code. Even in small things we will try not to compromise. We will not use the firm's photo-copier for private purposes; charge more overtime than we have actually worked; 'adjust' our mileage claims so as to claim more from our employer than we should do – or take similar 'accepted' perks. The moral individual will take a stand on principle and will not compromise. Such a position may be lonely and unpopular. Indeed friends and colleagues are likely to think us foolish if we do this as 'everyone does it'. For the moral individual, however, this is not a good argument. If something is wrong, the fact that many people do the action does not make it right.

This is a difficult and demanding path and is not easy to live by. It is not easy to take a stand on principle and to face the consequences. In the First and Second World Wars, some conscientious objectors (such as Quakers) refused to fight on moral grounds. They maintained that it was never right to kill people. They were openly derided in the streets, spat at, had white feathers (representing cowardice) given to them and were often put in prison. Nevertheless they took a stand because they believed that what they were doing was right.

A good example is that of an Austrian peasant farmer called Jaggerstater. Just before the Second World War, when Austria and Germany were politically united, the order went out that all farmers had to sell food they produced through the local Nazi-run market. Jaggerstater refused to agree because he maintained that the Nazis were evil. He had a wife and four children and his friends warned him of the consequences – nevertheless, he refused to compromise and would not sell any of his produce. Then, shortly afterwards, all men within a certain age range were called up into the armed forces. Again Jaggerstater refused to go – as he believed that the Nazis were evil. The mayor of the local town and his friends came to see him. They told him that if he did not obey he would be shot, his wife and children would lose the farm and he would have achieved nothing. After all, they said, he was only a peasant farmer and who would ever know? Jaggerstater refused. The mayor then said that he could get Jaggerstater a job in the hospital so that he could avoid the call-up. Again Jaggerstater refused – this would be a compromise and it was wrong. He would not compromise in any way. In due course the Nazis arrested him, and he was shot.

Jaggerstater had 'achieved' nothing – and yet he had remained true to what he believed in and had done what he considered was right. The consequences were for others to decide. Jaggerstater is a fine example of the moral individual, in love with 'the good'. He was a man that Socrates would have admired.

One of the problems of the moral life, is that it is not really clear as to what it is that is moral. Take the following examples:

a) Is homosexuality morally wrong?
b) Is abortion in certain circumstances permissible?
c) Is human embryo research morally justifiable?
d) Are nuclear weapons morally justifiable?
e) Is it right to trade with South Africa?

These are all questions where genuine and heated differences may arise between us. There is no obviously 'right' answer. It can, therefore, be difficult in the modern world to decide what is and what is not ethically 'right'. It is possible, therefore, for two people to attempt to live the moral life and to take two very different views on what constitutes the morally good.

Most of us never live our lives like this. We can, however, at least understand and admire such a person – even if we may regard him or her as foolish, impractical and unrealistic! The person living the moral life may well be a humanist or an atheist – God is not central. The person is 'in love' with goodness itself. Moral actions are not done for the hope of any reward and certainly not in the hope of praise from others or from fear of punishment. One thing alone motivates such a person – love of and commitment to goodness.

iv) *The religious life*
The person living the moral life has taken the decision to place morality at the centre of his or her life. Similarly if we live the religious life we take the decision to commit ourselves fully to a particular religion. It is a total commitment – but only up to a certain point. This may sound like

a contradiction, but it is not. The 'certain point' is the point of reason. We will commit ourselves fully to religion in so far as this does not offend against our reason or against reasonable conduct.

The religion that we may be committed to may be any religion represented by a Church or grouping of people within an institution – Buddhism, Hinduism, Islam, Judaism, Catholicism, Evangelical Christianity or any other that remains within the limits of human reason and where the emphasis is put on external observances. (It must be emphasised that not all the above religious groupings always place the emphasis on externals, but this does happen frequently.) The religious life represents an absolute commitment. If we are in love with religion we place religion at the centre of our life. It will always be of paramount importance. Because the commitment is absolute, it is that by which we judge all our actions or intentions.

In terms of the way we live, there will probably not be much difference between one of us who lives the religious life and one who lives the moral life – although it is possible that religious duties may be different from ethical duties. For instance, if one of us lives the religious life and is:

1) **A Catholic:** She may regard it as a duty to go to Mass, to make her confession; not to eat meat on Fridays; to have a devotion to the Virgin Mary; to believe the (few) proclaimed dogmas (such as the Assumption of the Virgin Mary and Papal Infallibility); to bring children up as Catholics, etc.

2) **A Jew:** He may regard it as a duty not to eat pork, only to marry another Jew, to have male children circumcised, to remain part of the Jewish community, to care for people within this community, not to work on a Saturday, to support the state of Israel, etc.

3) **A Muslim:** He may regard it as a duty not to eat pork, to read the Koran, to pray five times a day facing towards Mecca, to make a pilgrimage to Mecca at least once during his or her life, etc.

4) **A Hindu Brahman:** He may regard it as a duty to recognise cows as sacred, not to eat beef, never to harm any life if it can be avoided, once the needs of his family are satisfied to seek personal enlightenment, etc.

These duties are all external and objective. They are imposed on the individual by his adhering to a particular religion.

The religion a person follows may lay down moral rules which will differ between religions. A Catholic, for instance, might reject the possibility of artificial methods of birth control or abortion whilst a Muslim would be happy with four wives. In fact, traditional Catholic theology holds that in ethical matters the decision of each individual is, in the last analysis, final. Individual conscience reigns supreme – and this really means individual conscience, not conscience 'informed' or dictated to by the Church. Even St Thomas Aquinas and St Ignatius of Loyola maintained this position. It is rarely a stance that the Catholic Church proclaims clearly, though, and popular opinion does not always recognise it.

For any of us living the religious life, specific religious duties may rank equally with moral duties. These religious duties may separate those of us who centre our life on religion from those who are 'in love' with morality.

v) The Christian life
Given that most world religions can be fitted under the religious life, it may seem strange to have a fifth category. The religious life represented an absolute commitment – but only up to a certain point. That point was the limits

of human reason. Christianity, however, requires more
than this. *It requires faith in the paradox of Jesus Christ – the
God/man.* This is the absolute paradox which goes beyond
reason. It requires child-like trust in a personal, lived
relationship with God which comes before everything else,
yet goes beyond human understanding. The New Testament clearly recognised this:

> Love the Lord your God with all your heart, with all
> your soul and with all your mind. This is the greatest
> and most important commandment (Matt. 22:37–38).

There could not be a clearer definition. The Christian must
be 'in love' with God, putting his or her love relationship
with God before everything else. It is not for nothing that
in the ten commandments love of God is put first and that
Jesus describes this as 'the greatest and most important
commandment'. Today, many people make the second
commandment (love of neighbour) into the first and
relegate God to second place. If God came to earth out of
love for us, then the love of God must be central to the
Christian.

This does not mean that love of neighbour is not essential. None of us can claim to love God unless we have a
real, deep and practical care for and love of our fellow
man. This is not, of course, always easy – it is demanding
and sometimes uncomfortable, but it will flow inevitably
from a commitment to God. Its absence is a sure sign that
we have not begun to understand what loving God means.

Certainly the absolute paradox of Jesus, the God/man,
cannot be understood – but this is why faith is required,
the faith of a little child. Thus Jesus says:

> I assure you, that unless you change and become like
> little children, you will never enter the kingdom of
> heaven. The greatest in the kingdom of heaven is the

one who humbles himself and becomes like this little
child (Matt. 18:3–4).

Christianity is based on a love relationship with God
which, if it is real, will affect the whole of our lives. The
development of this relationship and bringing others to see
what it involves should be the central task of everyone who
calls themselves a Christian. Insofar as Church membership helps towards this (as it certainly should), well and
good. Once, however, outward observances and rituals
become a substitute for a personal love relationship then
they become a dangerous impediment to faith.

Rose Macaulay, the author of *Towers of Trebizond*, wrote
a letter to a friend in 1951 in which she put it this way:

> I don't attach much importantance to *details* of belief –
> I don't feel they really matter (or do they?). But I hold
> onto your remark: 'We may be sure that at the bottom
> of the whole business there is a personal relationship,'
> which is possibly all that matters. After what has
> occurred to me lately, I *know* there is . . .

Rose Macaulay, after a lifelong search, came to realise that
Christianity was founded on a love relationship with God.
Without even a dim awareness or search for this relation-
ship, we only have religion.

*

One day, we shall all die. Many people avoid thinking
about death – they find it frightening. One day I would
like to install a coffin in my college office for students to
sit on. Plato said that the philosopher should 'practice
dying' and after Roman banquets an empty coffin was
sometimes brought round for people to look at so that they
could be reminded of the inevitability of death. Death will
come to us all and it may come at any time. We need to

think about it beforehand and to consider how we shall cope.

When we come near to death, we may be in a hospital ward or at home, possibly in pain, waiting for our end. We may well have plenty of time to think back over our life and to consider how we have lived. It is important for us to think of that day well beforehand and to live in such a way that we can say 'no regrets' – we have lived as we wanted to. Each of us, if we believe in a life after death, will have to account for our life before God. We may well be asked on what we have centred our life, where our real treasure lay and what we were 'in love' with.

For those of us who claim to be Christians, we need to be aware of the distinction between the religious and the Christian life. The former can be tempting – it is comfortable and reassuring. We are one of a crowd and in a crowd there is always a feeling of security. The Christian life is much more challenging. It is, however, to the Christian life – the life in which we each, as individuals, find God and become aware of his love – that we are truly called. If we will only invest everything in God, if we will only depend totally on Him and commit ourselves into his care, then we do not need to worry about anything else. We will have found the only thing that really endures and we will have embarked on a relationship of love that begins in this life but continues after the grave.

Nothing – no opposition, no rejection, no worldly difficulties, no family troubles – can separate us from God's love. This love is found inside us as we seek to relate ourselves to God, but it will also transform our lives and the way we treat people.

There is a difference between love and being 'in love'. We can only be 'in love' with (or, in other words, 'absolutely committed to') one person or thing at a time – since this will be the centre point about which our whole life revolves. It can be worth asking:

1) *What or whom am I, as an individual, in love with or absolutely committed to at the present time, and*

2) *What or whom would I like to be in love with or absolutely committed to?*

There are five broad alternatives from which we can choose:

   i) *An unreflective life which has no direction or centre;*
   ii) *A life aimed at maximising pleasure, in various possible forms;*
   iii) *The moral life in which the main aim is to do 'the good';*
   iv) *The religious life;*
   v) *The Christian life centred on God.*

Each of us is free and we can make the choice for ourselves. We must consider the alternatives and the consequences and then decide on the absolute commitment to which everything else will take second place.

Christianity should involve putting the first commandment first and seeking and developing a love relationship with God before anything else. It really amounts to a love affair with God. God is placed at the centre of our lives and, because of this, the whole world is looked on in a new light. We should love our neighbour as ourselves and be 'in love' with God.

6

Abraham: Saint or Madman?

He: *People who really take Christianity seriously seem fanatical or intolerant. Some might even be described as mad.*

She: *What is madness?*

Being 'in love' involves centring our life on some person or purpose and thus represents an absolute commitment. It is absolute in that all other relationships and all other commitments are measured against it. We have looked at five possible alternative centres for life. The first, the unreflective life, was the life led by someone who does not have any clear focus or objective. External events dictate which way the person reacts. The second, the life devoted to pleasure, was seen to be attractive and led by many of us – but it is vulnerable to events outside our control and may not bring long term satisfaction.

Three possibilities remained – all requiring complete commitment and dedication. The ethical, the religious and the Christian lives. The ethical life gives total priority to goodness or virtue so that the person living it seeks to develop a 'good will' and to 'do good' in all circumstances. The religious life represents an absolute commitment to one or other of the world religions – in all cases this commitment remains within the limits of reason and concentrates on the externals of religion. Finally, the Christian commitment was seen to rest on a personal love relationship with God and the acceptance of the paradox of Jesus as both God and man. This is a move that faith alone can make and reason cannot get to grips with.

This may be all well and good, but what difference does it make? To what extent are there really any differences between the three positions? After all, all religions require obedience to a moral code. Between the moral and the religious centred life, there are likely to be the following major differences:

1) The life centred on religion will include observance of rituals required by the religion such as dietary laws, holding certain days or times as sacred, performance of recommended actions (e.g. pilgrimages or fasting) and attendance at religious services.

2) Differences in moral outlook (for instance in the realm of sexual behaviour)

3) Adherence to a religion is somewhat akin to belonging to a club. There are members and non-members of the club and membership of a religious group will give a feeling of 'belonging' which the moral individual may not have. The person whose life is centred on the ethical, by contrast, may see himself as doing the morally correct action and, in so doing, treating all men equally. There is no need to believe in gods or a life after death to be a moral person. There are many wonderful, loving and caring humanists.

There are a variety of different moral theories, but the one put forward by Kant is one of the clearest. He maintained that man's reason and morality are directly linked and that the moral demand was CATEG-ORICAL or absolute. There are various ways in which this was expressed, but these include:

i) Treat people always as ends, and never as means to
an end.
ii) Act so that the maxim of your action can be willed
to be a universal law.

For Kant, therefore, it is never permissible to use one
human being as a means to some wider end. Each individual person is tremendously important. Similarly,
when we come to consider our actions we should act in
such a way that we can truthfully will that anyone else,
in exactly the same position, should act as we are acting
(hence 'the maxim of your action can be willed to be a
universal law').

Kant provides an excellent grounding for a morality
that can be applied to everyone. Religious moralities
would have a good deal in common with this, but they
would sometimes appeal to the rulings of a Church
rather than to reason to decide which actions are and
which are not appropriate.

The religious and ethical way of life may, therefore, be
different but there are many similarities. There are also
many external similarities between the Christian (or God-
centred) life and the religious life. The reason for needing
to make the distinction between the Christian and religious
lives is that some priests and Church leaders (in all the
Churches) have, through the years, come to put too great
an emphasis on externals, thereby missing out the crucial
part of the Christian message. They have also, sometimes,
placed reason in first position – thus abolishing the paradox
of the God/man. Jesus himself recognised this would
happen when he condemned the pharisees and teachers
of the law for concentrating on the externals of religious
observances rather than an inner transformation of the
individual (Lk. 11:37–53). Again Jesus in Matthew 23
attacks the priests who concentrate on the externals. As an
example:

How terrible for you teachers of the law and Pharisees!
You hypocrites! You give to God a tenth even of the
seasoning herbs . . . but you neglect to obey the really
important teachings of the Law such as justice and mercy
(Matt. 23:23).

Those who go to Church and say 'Lord, Lord' every week
on Sunday will not be judged favourably because of this.
Again, for so many people it is the outward observances
that are important – they are living the religious life and
not the Christian life. Thus Jesus says that, at the final
judgement, many of those who expected to gain entry to
the Kingdom because they were religious will be rejected.
They will say, 'Open the door for us Sir!' But he will
reply, 'I don't know where you come from.' They will then
answer, 'We ate and drank with you; you taught in our
town.' To which Jesus will reply, 'I don't know where you
come from. Get away from me all you wicked people.' It
is not the externals of the religious life (such as taking
communion or taking part in the liturgy) that will be
decisive, but a lived relationship of love with God.

Almost all the major figures of the past have recognised
the love relationship with God as being at the heart of
Christianity and the major Churches have always rejected
the two heresies of seeing Jesus as only a man or as only
God. The early Councils of the Church (in which all the
leaders of the early Church met to define the Christian
faith and to preserve it against heresy) were also very
careful to say that Jesus is *both* God *and* man. This is not,
however, always taken as seriously as it might be at a local
level – hence the need to be clear on the difference between
the religious life and the Christian life.

There may, at times, be differences between the behaviour of someone living the religious and the Christian life
– although the most important difference will be internally.
To understand these possible differences it is helpful to
turn to the Old Testament story of Abraham.

*

Islam describes Christians, Jews and Muslims as 'The
People of the Book'. They all acknowledge the Old Testament as showing God's actions in history. All three
religions stress the importance of Abraham. Islam also
acknowledges the importance of Mary (with various refer-
ences to her in the Koran praising her purity and obedience) and it looks on Jesus as a prophet sent by God. In
contrast to the picture of militant Islam that we are given
in the West, the Koran actually says that the 'People of
the Book' have a great deal in common. Thus:

> . . . and dispute ye not with the people of the Book . . .
> but say 'We believe in the revelation which has come
> down to us and to you. Our God and your God is one
> and it is to Him that we bow' (5.29 art. 6).

To be sure, elsewhere in the Koran Muslims are exhorted
not to make friends of Jews and Christians, but the above
passage is nevertheless noteworthy.

The Jews look to Abraham as the father of Isaac and it
is from 'Father Abraham' and Isaac that Jews claim
descent. The Muslims look to Abraham as the father of
Ishmael (whose mother was Hagar, Sarah's slave girl). It
is Ishmael, not Isaac, who is given precedence in Islam
and they look to God's promise to make a 'great nation'
out of his descendants (Gen. 21:18). Christians regard
Abraham as the 'Father of faith' – acknowledged and
praised in the New Testament. Thus:

> Abraham believed God, and because of his faith, God
> accepted him as righteous . . . Abraham is the spiritual
> father of all who believe in God . . . God's promise is
> based on faith. Abraham believed and hoped even when
> there was no reason for hoping . . . (Romans 4).

The story of Abraham in the Old Testament MUST be
taken seriously – it cannot just be ignored or overlooked.

(Kierkegaard, in a marvellous and detailed study of the story of Abraham and Isaac [*Fear and Trembling* Princeton University Press and Penguin] spells out the lessons to be learnt.)

Abraham was called by God to sacrifice Isaac. Isaac was the son of Abraham's old age, conceived after Sarah had passed the menopause at a time when, therefore, conception should have been impossible. Isaac was Abraham's dearest treasure – his hope for the future. What is more, Abraham had been promised, through Isaac, descendants as numerous as the dust. Then, when Isaac was a young boy, God commanded Abraham to sacrifice Isaac. In other words, Abraham had to kill another human being – and not just any human being, but the dearest and closest person to him in the world. Abraham did not protest at all. He did not argue (although he had argued when God was going to destroy the cities of Sodom and Gomarrah. He persuaded God not to destroy the city first if there were fifty just men in the town; then forty-five; then forty; then thirty; then twenty and finally merely ten just men). Abraham was certainly prepared to argue with God on behalf of others, although he realised his own insignificance. He did not argue when it came to that which was the closest to him of all.

So Abraham set out for Mount Moriah, taking Isaac with him and the wood and live coals for the burnt offering. Imagine Abraham's feelings as he walked up the mountain, alone with his son – whom he knew he was about to kill. He could have thought various things:

1) He could have felt anger and fury at God but obeyed out of fear. In such a case, his relationship of trust would have been lost for ever – but he did not do this.

2) He could have felt resigned to the death of Isaac, accepting that God's promise of innumerable descendants through Isaac could not be fulfilled and regretful

that he had first believed and trusted in God – but he did not do this.

3) He could have refused and taken a stand on God's original promise. Effectively refusing to listen to God. According to reason, God was being ridiculous. He had made a promise and, if his promise was to be kept, he could not ask Abraham to kill Isaac. Rationally, Abraham had very good grounds for rejecting God's promise – but he did not do this.

4) Morally, to kill your son is totally unacceptable. Agreed, sacrifices were common in Canaan at the time of Abraham, but there is no evidence that Abraham practiced them, still less that the sacrifice of a son would be morally permissible. Abraham would have had strong moral grounds for rejecting God's command – but he did not do this.

Abraham believed. He trusted in his personal relationship with God. This relationship had called him out from Ur of the Chaldees and had led him throughout his life. It led him to believe that he would have a son in his old age, it led him to believe God's promises and to trust God in all things – and it led him at Mount Moriah to set out to sacrifice Isaac. Abraham believed, and he believed against the understanding because he believed two contradictory things:

1) He believed in God's promise that, through Isaac, he would have innumerable descendants, and

2) He believed that he would sacrifice Isaac.

These two beliefs cannot, rationally, be held at the same time. If 2) is true, then, rationally, 1) must be false. Abraham, however, believed that they were both true. Here we have another paradox – not the absolute paradox of Jesus the God/man, but a paradox nevertheless. A belief against the understanding is involved for the Christian and also, differently, for Abraham. Both positions only make sense in the light of faith and in the context of a living relationship with God.

Christianity demands a faith that goes beyond rationality. Reason and morality normally go together but, just occasionally, it is possible for a love relationship with God to cause someone to do something which goes against society's accepted moral norms. It may call one of us to leave mother and father, brothers and sisters for a higher love.

If we centre our lives on morality, then our intellect will reign supreme. In the Christian life, lived as part of a love relationship with God, it is just possible that this relationship might call an individual to act against what appears to be rational, reasonable and understandable. For the moral life, the interests of the largest number of people must come first. For Christianity, the person in relationship with God may actually be more important than the crowd. We do not know the consequences of our action and the Christian will, after prayer and reflection, do what he or she feels called to do – and leave the consequences to God.

It is very difficult to determine the effects which our actions will have. A student of mine at the Institute of Education brought in a story of a scientifically documented 'miracle' which happened to a man called Traynor. As a result, I used this same example in an introductory book on philosophy of religion (*God of our Fathers?* DLT, 1987). So because one person brought in an article, this same article achieved circulation not just in this country but overseas and the consequences of this cannot be measured. As another example, a priest had an affair with a friend of mine and, as a result, the friend's neighbours were put off Christianity. Our actions are like a stone thrown into a pond – we cannot tell what happens to the ripples. They may harm or strengthen people we have never even known.

The idea that Christianity may possibly call us outside the norms of society is a dangerous and frightening position and it needs to be approached with extreme care. Normally, for us to do something that we cannot fully understand or rationalise or to act against society's conventions is simply wrong whether we centre our lives on morality, religion or a relationship with God. Thus to commit murder, to steal, to covet, etc. are all evils to be avoided. They are all self-centred. We must seek to do away with self-interest and to love others. Morality is almost universally understood and accepted (at least within a particular society). Few of us actually do live a good moral life, but we can all understand it.

Possibly, however, if we are really trying to relate our life wholly to God, we can be called to act against society's norms. We can be called to obey God and not the crowd. This was what Abraham was called to do. It might, of course, be reasonable to say that Abraham was mad. Peter Sutcliff, for instance, was supposedly told by God in a graveyard to go out and murder prostitutes – and he did. There is a fine dividing line between the person who obeys what he sees as his duty to God and someone who is mad. There are, however, ways of separating the two. Abraham's call from God came towards the end of a life of faith dedicated to a relationship with God – the same cannot be said of Sutcliff.

Morally, Abraham is a person who intended to commit murder and he must be discounted. Professor Keith Ward, of King's College, London, takes this view. Morally, Keith Ward is right. Morally, Abraham is mad. Morally, what Abraham set out to do was to commit murder; from a Christian point of view it was to obey God. The lived relationship with God can call one of us beyond the ethical. Such a call is a frightening and dangerous one and anyone who thought they had such a call would have to seriously consider whether they were, in fact, mad. (Incidentally the ability to ask this question is sometimes one of the grounds for affirming sanity!) More commonly, the Christian may be called on to reject the norms of society – to reject materialism and self-seeking, to question the values of a society which measures success largely in financial terms and where compassion and self-giving is considered as odd.

One of the worst features of trying to live out a relationship with God is that one may not be able to make anyone else understand – it can be very lonely and hard. It is much more demanding than most people who call themselves Christians would ever dream. Abraham was in this position – he has to be silent about God's command. Who could he talk to – Sarah? She could not have understood and would never have allowed the sacrifice of her only son. His slaves? They could neither understand nor help. Isaac? Impossible. The nature of Abraham's relationship with God demands silence (as most Christian spiritual writers affirm – few of them are willing to speak about their relationship with God. In fact, this relationship is something that cannot be spoken about directly).

In my college, there was recently a bright and attractive twenty-three-year-old girl who studied under me. She was full of life, loved meeting people and was always interested in Christianity – challenging the assumptions and thinking through issues for herself. We talked from time and time and I came to know her a little better. To my great surprise, she started to consider the possibility of entering a religious order and was 'shopping around' for the one she felt would be right for her. Eventually she settled on the Carmelites – a choice I could not understand as they are largely enclosed and contemplative. Her vitality and youth seemed to fit badly with the image I had of this particular community.

She gave me a book called *The Way of a Pilgrim* (Image Books) written by a nineteenth-century Russian monk. From reading this and from small hints that had been dropped indirectly, from comments she had made about friends and from things her friends had mentioned to me, I gradually came to see the depth that lay beneath the surface. Beneath the bright sunny exterior was a growing and deep commitment to a love relationship with God that put everything else into second place. She never talked about this, but she nevertheless communicated indirectly. Whether I or anyone else would understand was left open. Many of her friends would call her mad.

She would be giving up the possibility of an intimate relationship with a man, children and family life, freedom to travel, the chance of a rewarding career, many friends, the pleasures of a great deal of the modern world and putting in its place the cloister. What is more, it would not be just any cloister but a totally enclosed order which no one from outside would ever enter. Instead of living and working as a Christian within the world, she would be opting for a relationship with God alone. Most people would say she was crazy or personally inadequate. She could not prove that she was not mad and would certainly admit her personal inadequacies – but not in the way that the outside world thought. She had found a relationship with God which put the whole world into a new light.

I once asked this girl if she had been asked whether she was being selfish. 'Frequently', she said. Her reply to them was this: 'I am part of the Church – just a small part, but a part nevertheless. If one is going to specialise, one needs to devote all one's efforts to it – whether one is going to be a doctor, a teacher or an accountant. I feel God is calling me to be a specialist in love through a life of prayer, detachment, chastity and obedience. Some people may not understand, but I must be faithful to my own conscience . . .'

Abraham had to keep silence. Talking to others would have blunted the challenge of faith and they could not understand. If Abraham had talked, he would have been persuaded that he was acting unreasonably – that he should ignore the test. Talking can itself be a temptation as other individuals will always try to lessen the demands that God makes to something that human reason can understand and human weakness can cope with. There are real dangers in talking at times – and the story of Abraham shows one of them.

This is not, of course, to rule out discussion. Thus my twenty-three-year-old former student would herself have close friends she could go to. Spiritual advisers or fellow pilgrims on the road to faith can be a support and an inspiration. In the final analysis, however, each individual must stand alone. We may recognise and seek guidance and help from fellow travellers, but the decisions must be ours.

Any Church which aims to bring its members closer to God, to try to transform their lives so that they are aware of God's presence at all times and to change their whole outlook on the world so that they show real love for others is a Christian Church. Regretfully, this is not always the case – many priests in all Churches concentrate on the externals and the need for inner transformation is ignored.

It might seem that Mother Teresa in Calcutta would be another example of someone living the Christian life but this is not necessarily the case. Mother Teresa *could* be living the religious or the Christian life. The love relationship with God cannot be judged by external actions. Mother Teresa very probably is living the Christian life – she may, or may not, have a relationship with God. No one besides herself can tell. No person can, therefore, judge another. Each of us needs to be concerned about our own position and should avoid judging others. We can look to admirable figures such as Mother Teresa as an inspiration, but we each have our own path to follow and the big question for each of us is: Are we following our path to God with total commitment and dedication?

The religious life and the Christian life may be distinct. The story of Abraham can help to pinpoint the difference. The Christian life is based on a love relationship with God. It is just possible that this relationship may call us to act against the normal standards of our society. It is possible that outsiders will consider us foolish or even mad. This is a lonely and terrifying position to be in. The individual relating wholly to God may sometimes find communication with others difficult. He or she will have accepted the absolute paradox and therefore moved beyond reason in a simple and child-like faith based on commitment to and love of God.

7

Detachment
and living in the world

He: *I'm considering buying a new Volvo. Do you know anything about them? The Vauxhall is also a possibility – it's not easy to decide.*

She: *Have another cup of coffee.*

Christianity involves putting the first commandment first, but how does this relate to the rest of life? If it is accepted that we are called into a love relationship with God, what effects will this have on the way we lead our lives? These practical questions are vital. Unless Christianity is a religion that can be lived, that the ordinary person can at least try to live out, then it is irrelevant in the latter part of the twentieth century.

When it is claimed that Christianity calls us into a love relationship with God, it is important to be clear on what this means. Obviously it assumes the existence of a personal, living God who is capable of love. The word 'love' needs to be understood in a broadly similar manner to the way it is used on earth, although obviously God's love far exceeds ours. For a start, human love falters. God's love is, however, unchanging. It is the same yesterday, today and tomorrow and, no matter what we do, God will still love us. God will, however, respect our free decision as to whether we wish to love him in return. That, after

all, is why we are on this earth – to make a decision for or
against God.

Some people, of course, never get to know God's reality
– they have no use for the idea of God. This, strangely
enough, need be no bar to loving God. God can be loved
and cared for in the human people around us and if this
love is intense and dedicated enough, we will become the
same sort of person as we might have become through
combining love of God with love of neighbour. Love has a
power to transform us and, whilst Christianity envisages
love of God coming first and love of neighbour arising from
this, it has always accepted that some may 'love much'
without being aware of God.

Jesus refers to those who will enter the heavenly kingdom
and who never knew that they loved God. They cared for
Him, however, by caring for the destitute, the poor, the
sick and those in prison (Matt. 25:44–46). The pious, those
people leading the dedicated 'religious life' and going to
Church regularly and participating in all the Church
services, may well be rejected because their religion was
not based on love – either of God or of other people.
Anyone who claims that they love God and then really
does not love those that they meet in their everyday life,
cannot understand what it is to love. Love is not at all
easy.

Why, however, love God? There can be no easy answer
to this question. We are not drawn to love God because
He created the world and is omnipotent and omniscient.
There is more to it than this. It is partly a question of
coming to recognise something that is worthy of single-
minded love and is immensely attractive and desirable.

There are very few things in life that any of us can seek
single-mindedly – in other words there are few objectives
that we can devote ourselves to for themselves alone. It is,
of course, easy to be double-minded about a relationship
with God. One may seek to love Him out of fear of possible
punishment. In other words, fear of 'hell-fire' may push us

towards God. It is difficult to generate love out of fear, however, although we *do* need to recognise that if Christianity is true, the way we live our lives has consequences. Some people have been brought up to fear God above everything else. As children, they are in terror of God as a judge who will be angry with them if they do not perform certain duties laid down by their religion. This is not Christianity – it is a life based on duties and obligations rather than relationships and is a feature of the 'religious life'. It is still, alas, all too common a feature in some churches.

It is also possible to seek to love God because we hope for a reward in heaven if we do so. Imagine that you meet someone whom you really begin to care for. You like them a great deal and enjoy spending time in their company. You invite them to spend an evening with you – but why? There are two possible answers to this. Firstly one might say 'I am doing this for a reason.' For instance, you may want to seduce the person and the evening will have been wasted if the objective is not achieved. To seek to love anyone, most of all God, out of hope of a reward is not truly love and it mistakes the nature of the possible 'reward'.

The second possible reason for spending time in the person's company is simply because you enjoy their company. There is no ulterior motive whatsoever. In this case, the evening cannot be wasted, since what is valued is the person's company. In the parallel case of God, this is a matter of loving God for Himself and for the sake of the relationship alone. The hymn-writer sums up the position well:

> *O Lord I love Thee not because I hope for heaven thereby*
> *Nor yet for fear that loving not I may for ever die.*

The relationship of love begun with God before death is, the Christian believes, continued after death. If, therefore, the single objective that we seek beyond everything else (in other words that to which we are 'absolutely comitted' or that which we are 'in love' with) is a lived love relationship with God, then death becomes as nothing. The relationship exists before and after death – death has been overcome and is of no significance. Instead, therefore, of having to think in terms of heaven and hell with wine, women and song on the one hand and devils' tails amongst the flaming furnaces on the other, there can be a picture of:

1) Those who, in this life, have chosen the path of a relationship with God: this would continue after death, except that it would be more complete and full than was ever possible on earth. We would come to know God fully and to be in His presence, and

2) on the other side, those who have refused the offer of love, who have refused to respond with love and refused to make themselves into individuals who can love. They will have exiled themselves from any wish for a relationship with God. That is their choice – they are free, and their decision must be respected.

Today, there are a significant number of people who call themselves Christians, particularly amongst the more sophisticated clergy and theologians, who:

a) are agnostic (i.e. unsure about) any life after death. They may consider that Jesus did not really rise from the tomb and that Christianity is simply a matter of calling people to a good, ethical life, and

b) maintain that, if there is a life after death, then everyone will be 'saved' and treated equally.

I have yet to discover any intellectual grounding for either of these views. They seem to be based on a Western, liberal 'feeling of the times' as to what is or is not acceptable.

Neither view has any real support in the history of Christianity.

Now it may be that Christianity is untrue – this has to be a possibility. Perhaps Jesus (there is no doubt there was such a person) was deluded. Perhaps many of the stories about him were made up or were later embellishments to true stories about one of the wandering prophets of the time. *If*, however, Jesus is the person that the Christian Church has always claimed Him to be, *if* he is fully God and fully man, then there not only seems to be no implausibility at all in His having risen from the dead but, also, His promise that all mankind would rise and be judged individually seems perfectly credible.

If Jesus is God, he would presumably have ensured, by whatever means He chose, that the New Testament provided a sound view of His teachings. This does not mean that every word was dictated by God. The Bible was written by human beings and Bible scholars can tell us much about its origins and help us to understand it. It does mean, however, that (*if* Jesus is the God/man), the Bible can be broadly relied upon. (Samuel Taylor Coleridge in *Confessions of an Enquiring Spirit* has possibly one of the most credible views on biblical inspiration and his book is well worth reading.)

If this life is *not* a matter of each of us making a decision about what sort of person to become, if we are *not* free to choose to respond to God or to reject Him, and if we do *not* have to take the consequences of our free decisions, then if there *is* a God it seems that we must be in an obscene world. Millions suffer and die on earth – an explanation for the problem of evil is outside the scope of this book – and if there is no after-life and if our choices here do not matter, then the problem of evil seems insurmountable.

Christianity claims that each of us can move towards a relationship of love with God and our fellow human beings. This relationship can start on this earth and will continue after death. This does not explain, however, how the love relationship can be lived out in the world.

There is no single, outward form of the Christian life. Goodness and holiness are not external features. They are internal qualities which may, nevertheless, be recognisable. Almost no job or task in life is barred to the Christian. The love relationship can be lived out down a mine, on a production bench, in a banker's office, as a civil servant, as a teacher or a housewife. There are, however, some areas of life where it may be much more difficult, if not impossible. Examples include:

1) It would not be possible to be a guard in a death camp, a torturer of prisoners or a professional assassin and still claim a relationship of love with God. There are, therefore, a small group of 'professions' that seem, of themselves, to rule out a love relationship, although the number of obvious instance is limited.

2) Some professions can make it difficult to be true to the love relationship. These *might* include, for instance, being a politician or journalist since both professions *can* make it difficult to be true to yourself. The politician or journalist has to appeal to the mass of people, they have to get elected or sell their articles. A politician with real, honest and upright principles can find his position a very difficult one. He or she has to gain selection as a candidate, abide by party whips if elected, get re-elected on a manifesto that he or she did not draft and remain a loyal party member. This can impose very real strains.

3) Jobs which require any of us to be so busy that time for prayer and for God is ruled out, can make a real relationship with God almost impossible. Any relationship needs to be fostered and built up. This requires quiet, prayer and an increasing awareness of God's presence. A person would have to have very great depth to

be able to maintain this awareness in the hectic rush of a stock-broker's office. It is not impossible – only difficult.

4) The more successful we become, the more difficult it can be to be aware of God. Firstly there are the time pressures, but more important material concerns constantly intrude. We cannot serve God and mammon. Either the interests of God or the interests of making money must be put at the centre of our lives. Life can only have one centre and if this centre is God, then time and effort devoted to the acquisition of material prosperity is likely to seem time wasted. To be a successful businessman or woman demands time, dedication, concentration and effort. It is almost impossible to devote these energies to business success and yet to centre one's life on God and the love of all the people one meets.

To be sure, the successful man or woman may 'find time for God', but this is not what a love relationship entails. It involves moving God out from the centre place to the periphery of our lives. If our whole effort and thought is given to developing our love relationship and bringing other people to it as well, then commitment to business success is likely to be small indeed.

Christianity requires passion. A love relationship with no passion is almost a contradiction in terms. Passion, dedication to the relationship and commitment is required so that each of us seeks to build our lives round a relationship with God. Everything else takes second place to this.

The committed Christian may well go incognito. Nothing obvious may be seen externally. He or she may be like the person next door except that, inwardly, material concerns will not be a high priority. Time centred on the material is time taken away from the person's relationship with God and from bringing others to see the importance of this relationship. This does *not* mean that the Christian needs to go around in sackcloth and ashes. Indeed any outward show or ostentation needs to be avoided as it switches the emphasis away from the inner to the outer.

It is easy to become concerned with outward appearances whilst, in reality, these are of little significance. The concentration on 'church' and external appearances is one of the features of the religious (as opposed to the Christian) life. It is the inner transformation resulting from the relationship with God that is central, and any job or task in life that does not get in the way of this is perfectly possible.

When considering Abraham we saw that he was in a lonely position. He could not make others understand him. The same may well happen to many people trying to live the Christian life. They will be surrounded by the crowd, the mass of people, most of whom are living an unreflective life. Popular opinions and taste hold sway and anyone really trying to take Christianity seriously will be in an isolated position. Few people today understand a religious perspective on life at all and, to the extent that it is understood, it is thought of in external terms. The idea of anyone trying to live a love relationship with God is likely to be considered fanatical, unrealistic, unnecessary and, perhaps, simply mad. It is significant that, in the Soviet Union, many evangelical Christians used to be placed in hospitals for the mentally ill.

Each of us who tries to take this path will, therefore, find ourselves forced back onto the relationship with God – depending entirely on Him and seeking comfort from Him alone. There may, to be sure, be fellow pilgrims along the road and these can provide encouragement and an awareness of being one of many people trying to live this sort of life. We can draw strength and help from the Christian community and the knowledge that we are all part of a universal, Christian Church which spans the globe as well as the centuries. We cannot take refuge in the crowd, however; we need to find God for ourselves, although others will help us in the search and we, in turn, must help others along the road. It can be a difficult and stony path and we all need support as we journey.

It seems difficult to understand the reasoning behind an individual's decision to move from one church to another. Cardinal Newman commented just before he left the Anglican Church for Rome that, should he die that night, he would not have felt that his soul was safe as an Anglican. This is to imply that Church labels matter to God. What is of paramount importance is not, surely, the label we wear but the extent to which we try to live up to the relationship with God.

We can draw nearer to God (or be just as far away from Him) in any Church. It is the passion and commitment with which we seek Him and with which we show His love in our lives that matters, not the clothes we have on. We are able to draw closer to God within almost any Church community, and we may feel that one community may make this easier for us than others. This may, sometimes, have more to do with the local church leaders than to denominational labels. Some people prefer one type of worship, some another. Whatever the form of worship, however, the objectives should be the same.

Recognising Jesus as both God and man, accepting that this human individual was the son of God who created the Universe, the second person of the Trinity, is the first step in a new relationship. It may well be described as a 'new birth'. Christians sometimes refer to baptism as a 'New Birth', but this can be misleading.

A man and woman make love, nine months later a baby may be born, shortly thereafter a few drops of water are sprinkled and Lo! a Christian 'saved soul' is meant to result. We have the essential truth of Christianity transformed into a ritual sometimes undertaken for its own sake. People who never darken the doors of a church will nevertheless come to have their baby 'done'. For most people, they have no real idea why they are doing it, but it is considered the 'right thing to do'. It may well be regarded as an insurance policy for eternity.

John the Baptist baptised adults and it was an outward sign of an inner transformation that the individual was accepting for himself. It was a sign of a new birth and a new beginning. Once an individual has actually come to understand, for him or herself, what Christianity involves, then, like the dots which make up a picture, the knowledge is there. The world shifts its focus. Instead of this world and its materialistic priorities being the essential reality, suddenly God's love and the love of our fellow man is seen as the ultimate and this new vision puts most of the rest of human striving into the shade. Our perspective alters and the alteration is permanent – it represents a time of illumination.

This should not be seen as denying the value, in some Churches, of infant baptism. Baptism marks the entry of a child into the Christian community – but all Churches accept that this is only the first step. Churches that practice infant baptism follow this with Confirmation so that the child, when he or she is older, can make the decision for him or herself.

To be sure, even if we have come to understand what a relationship with God calls us to, we may choose to ignore the call. The price of a positive response is costly and many of us will turn away. Baptism may well be an appropriate mark of this new vision, of the new birth, but it does not, of itself, change the individual. God's love is extended to everyone – it is not conditional on baptism.

Once we have seen what Christianity involves, once we have accepted that Jesus is both God and Man and have decided to 'take this on board', then the task of life can begin: to try to live out the relationship with God. This is most extraordinarily difficult, but it is also easy! At the beginning, it can be hard enough to have a relationship with a God whom we can neither see, touch or feel. Indeed there will be many times when even to talk of a relationship with God seems to verge on the absurd. Once we have decided to set out in search of God, however, then all the normal burdens and troubles of life fall away and lose their significance. This is why Jesus says that the burden he offers is easy – it only requires total love and commitment. If this step will only be taken, everything else falls into place.

If we have a friend, we will enjoy being in his or her presence and talking to the person. Talking is not, however, always necessary. One of the marks of a true friendship is that we can be quiet – spending time in the person's company without having to fill the silence with banalities. So it is with God. Prayer should be a pleasure rather than a burden or duty. Too often, however, prayer is seen as 'talking at' God rather than simply living in the presence of God. As we become more aware of God's presence in our lives, so everything that we can do should become part of our prayer. Our lives start to be lived in an awareness of God. John Wesley put it this way:

> God's command to *pray without ceasing*, is founded on the necessity . . . to preserve the life of God in the soul . . . Whether we think of or speak of God, whether we act or suffer for him, all is prayer, when we have no other object than his love, and the desire of pleasing him.
>
> All that a Christian does, even in eating or sleeping, is prayer, when it is done in simplicity, according to the order of God. (*A Plain Account of Christian Perfection.*)

The final result of a life dedicated to God is a life of prayer – not in the sense of 'talking at' God all the time, but being continually aware of God's presence. In the *Spiritual Diary* of St Ignatius of Loyola, as well as in the works of other mystical writers, there is an awareness that the first stage of a relationship with God may indeed involve prayer, remorse for past mistakes and similar features. At a later stage, however, this gives away to a simple awareness of God's presence. The road to God is a long one, and there are different features as we progress on the road – but being aware of His presence in some fashion is central to all of them.

It would require a separate book to even begin to set out the steps on the ladder towards God. In fact, it is a process that each of us must go through for ourselves. Certainly reading the writings of others who have taken the road can help. In a love relationship, however, only so much talking or reading is useful – the most effective tutor is actually to try out the relationship for oneself.

One necessary step, however, is a detachment from material concerns and priorities. This is, again, a painful process. Most of us realise our identity through our possessions and our status in life. Our car, the size of our office, our job title, our marital status, our house, the furniture we own all make statements about us. They all proclaim 'This is me!' Anyone who challenges us in these areas, challenges our individuality.

When one of us loses our job or gets divorced, we feel devalued, debased, unwanted and a failure. It often takes a prolonged period of healing for us to come to 'like ourselves' again. Having been rejected by an employer, a spouse or anyone else can make us feel inadequate.

There is an accepted 'classification ritual' that most of us run through when we meet someone. This classification process is often subtle, but it rests on acquiring certain pieces of information. For instance:

- What is your career or job? Whom do you work for?
- How much do you earn (although this is never asked directly)?
- What car do you drive?
- Are you married, single or divorced?
- What social group do you belong to? Where did you go to school?

To God, none of these questions matter in the slightest. We came into the world with nothing, and we shall go out of it the same way. The status, possessions and paraphernalia with which we clutter our lives will all have to be disposed of. We can take with us through death our relationship with God and our love of others, nothing more. Wealth, education, social position and possessions are all irrelevant. It follows that, if we really want to begin a relationship with God, we need to detach ourselves from all those things that seem so important to the vast majority of people. Suddenly, they count for very little.

It is, of course, frightening to strip ourselves of all those things which define who we are. A friend of mine who is a former Benedictine monk says that he looks on confession as going naked before God. For most of us, our naked bodies are not a very pleasant sight. Without our clothes on, we can be seen as we really are – our muscles sag in the wrong places and our defences are down. When we are really trying to develop a relationship with God, we need to see ourselves without the façade that others see and which we so carefully keep around us like a shield to hide our true selves.

It follows from this that the committed individual will gradually become detached from the things of this world. Our lives should not really be centred here. Such an individual will have found the treasure of great price and the wish to deepen the relationship with God will come before everything else. To be sure, such a person will live this life to the full, but in terms of priorities, he or she will be detached from most material concerns and will consider them of little significance. Financial loss or gain, a promotion or demotion, the purchase of a new video recorder, microwave or car or even of a new house may not be cause for major pleasure or regret. Measured against the permanence of the relationship with God, they are all likely to appear shallow.

C.S. Lewis recognised the problem clearly. In *Mere Christianity* he writes as follows:

> The terrible thing, the almost impossible thing, is to hand over your whole self – all your wishes and precautions – to Christ. But it is far easier than what we are all trying to do instead. For what we are trying to do is to remain what we call 'ourselves', to keep personal happiness as our great aim in life and yet at the same time to be 'good'. We are all trying to let our mind and heart go their own way – centred on money or pleasure or ambition – and hoping, in spite of this, to behave honestly and chastely and humbly.
>
> And that is exactly what Christ warned us you could not do. As He said, a thistle cannot produce figs. If I am a field that contains nothing but grass-seed, I cannot produce wheat . . . If I want to produce wheat, the change must go deeper than the surface. I must be ploughed up and re-sown.

We cannot hold onto our own identities and interests which are centred on the world and take on Christianity as well. We need to become detached from the world in order to be transformed by the relationship with God.

People will come to matter far more to us than things. Our possessions will become of less and less significance and, in their place, our relationships with others will take first priority. It will be in caring for and loving others that we show our love of God.

The letter to the Romans expresses this position well:

> Do not conform yourselves to the standards of this world, but let God transform you inwardly by a complete change of your mind. Then you will be able to know the will of God – what is good and is pleasing to Him and is perfect (Romans 12:2).

Once we have genuinely centred our lives on God and become detached from the things of this world, the way is open for following Christ and the development of the love relationship.

Imagine a young man who comes from a very wealthy family. His father is an international businessman. He is well educated and his parents are generous – he is given a flat of his own and is able to spend time in his parents' house in South Africa, at their house in Surrey and in his own flat. His life stretches before him and he has to decide what to do. He may have been brought up as a Christian and goes to Church regularly.

He goes to university and begins to think through his faith for the first time. He finally comes to the conclusion, for himself and not just based on what he has been taught, that Jesus *is*, indeed, God. Christianity *is* true. He becomes aware of God's presence – although there are few people to whom he can explain this. He continues to mix in his parents' world of smart dinners, the theatre and the opera. He is now faced by a problem – what should he do with his life?

His parents may want him to be a lawyer and this is something that all his friends would understand. He would follow in the steps of his successful father. The appeal of this is considerable. 'Surely', he may say to himself, 'I can be a successful businessman, enjoy the pleasant life style I am accustomed to and still be a Christian?'

The question he has to ask himself is whether this is really a possibility. *Can* he really fit in with his family's expectations and still be a committed Christian? Can he drive his Porsche past the corrugated iron shanty town in which children play in the mud and have not enough to eat on his way to play tennis on the family's tennis court in their Johannesburg home? Only he can, in the end, decide but if he does not at least ask whether something more may be required of him, then he is not taking God seriously.

Anyone who seriously believes that we are made for fellowship with God, that we shall survive death and there be judged by the way we have lived our lives will, necessarily, look on life in a different way. Joy in the world is still, of course, possible – but the joys and sorrows need to be looked at from an altered perspective, from a viewpoint that is not limited to our three score years and ten.

A relationship of love with God needs to be sought for itself alone and not as a means to any other end. This relationship, the Christian believes, can start in this life and will continue after death. Death should, therefore, be of no importance to us at all. We must decide in this life whether we will choose for or against love and our decision will be respected after we die. Either we can choose to make ourselves people who can love and who can accept love, or we can turn away. The choice is ours.

If we choose to centre our lives on God, then we will tend to become detached from material concerns. Instead people will matter to us and it is in our care and love for them that we shall show our love of God.

8

Friends and Enemies

He: *My boss is a bastard. He's off to Tenerife with his girl friend next week thank goodness. We can get some work done in the office. I've got to have him to dinner when he gets back. That will be a pain.*

She: *Did I ever tell you about my friend Anne? She's just flown into the war zone near Juba to work in a school there.*

Each of us is free, although it may not be easy to actually make use of this freedom. Social and parental expectations, schooling, the environment in which we live and our friends all pressurise us to conform and to live according to society's expectations. Resisting these pressures is not easy. One of the best and truest ways in which one of us can help another is to encourage them to use their freedom – to bring them out of the darkness of their 'programming' which their background has imposed. We can stand on our own feet and decide for ourselves what to do with our lives.

It follows from this that, once we have made our own, free decision about how to live, this is a matter for us alone. It is no concern of anyone else to say that we are 'wrong' or 'foolish' – *provided* we have clearly thought through our choice of life and its consequences. Loving other people, really caring for them as true friends, means putting their happiness first and if they have a different perspective on life then, although this may be a cause for regret, this is their decision and will not affect our love for them.

True friendship is rare. The word 'friend' like 'love' is over used. A true friend will care for his friend whatever happens. Many friendships are based on selfishness – each party giving in proportion to what is received. One person meets another and the 'chemistry works', the relationship holds out the promise of something deeper. The exploration process then begins with each side revealing more and more about him or her self and becoming more vulnerable to the other. Many so-called friendships remain at a superficial level, concealed behind a mask of pretence with neither side willing to reveal themselves for what they really are – aware of their own shortcomings and the likely effect of these on the other.

As both sides reveal more and more of themselves, the likelihood of disappointment increases. Real friendship, however, occurs when we can accept someone else as they are, warts and all, and still care and love in the same way. Love could well be defined as friendship carried to the highest degree – a total acceptance and care for the other and a willingness to put ourselves in second place to our friend. A true friend will never 'use' the other and will care to such an extent that helping and listening is always a pleasure and not a burden.

When we have a friend, we will care for him or her. We will obviously be concerned if our friend has not seen something which is most important of all to us. If, therefore, we try to live the ethical, religious or Christian life and have a friend who has not thought about life at all (and who is, therefore, living the unreflective life) or who has dedicated his or her life to pleasure, we will naturally be concerned. The concern will not be to impose our will on the other but, out of love for the friend, to help them see what they have so far missed.

If, having talked together and reflected, our friend does not want to change the way that life is lived, then that is his or her free decision and must be respected. It will certainly not affect our love for and care of the individual.

Genuine friendship represents a commitment and is costly. It will involve the investment of time and the risk, at least as the friendship develops, of being misunderstood and rebuffed. Certainly it will involve putting self in second place. Sören Kierkegaard, the Danish philosopher and theologian to whose writings I owe so much, fell completely in love with a young girl, Regine Olsen, when he was a young man. They courted and became engaged; but Kierkegaard reflected on his forthcoming marriage and came to the conclusion that he could not make Regine happy. It was partly because he felt called to a particular task in life which was likely to make him unpopular, but also from his considered view of his somewhat melancholy character. But he loved her tremendously. If he had tried to explain to her his reasons for having doubts about the marriage, she would have assured him of her love and devotion and would have remained even more firmly committed to him. Kierkegaard loved her so much that he came to the conclusion that he could not allow this – he had to break the engagement, but he had to do it in such a way that would leave Regine emotionally free from him so that she could seek happiness elsewhere. He therefore broke the relationship in a cold and hard manner. Regine could not understand and was bitterly unhappy. She soon got over it, however, and within six months was married to a former teacher of hers.

Kierkegaard remained in love with Regine throughout his life. So much was this so that one glance from her in church on a Sunday some years later disconcerted him to such an extent that he felt he had to leave the country and go to Berlin for a time. When he died, he left her everything he had, although she did not accept it.

Here we have an example of self-giving love carried to the extent of really putting self-interest in second place to the good of the beloved. It is, unfortunately, all too rare.

The person whom we marry should, ideally, be our best friend – the person with whom we can share everything; all the most important parts of our personality. If we really love someone, we will be interested in him, in all those things that are important to him and we will share his concerns, if not for our own sake then for his. To say that we love someone and not to be interested in him (or her) as an individual, is a denial of love. It is to keep ourselves aloof and apart. I once heard a young man say to his new wife, 'I'm not interested in knowing about your background or what happened before I met you – only the future is important.' This, however, betrays a lack of love and commitment. It is one thing to say that we are not concerned about a person's past (which may possibly have been troubled and difficult), but just to dismiss someone's background as unimportant is to fail to take them seriously.

It is partly for this reason that similar outlooks on life are important when considering marriage – if someone who is a committed Christian and wants to centre his life on God and care of neighbour, marries an atheist, their love will have to be particularly strong to overcome the difficulties that are bound to arise because of a lack of shared perception of the world and priorities for life. Love can overcome these difficulties – our love for another should not depend on beliefs – but it becomes much harder the more the outlooks of the two partners have different centres. If two people who live with each other have centred their lives in totally different ways, strains are likely to arise. The priorities of the one partner will not be shared with or even understood by the other.

Difficult as it may be to have real friends and to genuinely love other people to whom we are naturally attracted, the problem becomes even greater if we try to have the same commitment to people to whom we are not drawn, or to whom we feel indifferent or even dislike. To actually 'love your enemies', to put our interests in second place to theirs, to give them our jacket if they try to steal our coat, to let them strike us on both cheeks if they first strike us on one, seems almost impossible. This is, however, what the Christian life calls us to.

Unreasonable though this may seem at first, it is perfectly sensible. If God, indeed, exists and if he loves every one of us, then every single individual, no matter how hard or unpleasant, is a person whom God cares about and loves and with whom God seeks a personal relationship. From God's side, the hand of friendship is always outstretched, but man constantly turns away. It is, therefore, up to every person who aspires to live the Christian life to try to show others the love of God. As we have seen, 'talking at' people is unlikely to be successful. Indirect communication is needed, and this is best achieved by loving and caring for every individual we come across, really being interested in them, as individuals. Effectively, the Christian is called to love everyone – not in an abstract or impersonal way, but in a manner that amounts to genuine friendship, even though the relationship may be one way only. C.S. Lewis in *Mere Christianity* put it this way:

> Do not waste time bothering whether you 'love' your neighbour; act as if you did. As soon as you do this we find one of the great secrets. When you are behaving as if you loved someone, you will presently come to love him. If you injure someone you dislike, you will find yourself disliking him more. If you do him a good turn, you will find yourself disliking him less.

For most of us, it is hard enough to selflessly love those to whom we are attracted. The call to widen the circle of friends to include those whom we do not find congenial is a massive task. Lewis shows that we can change our feelings for people by acting towards them in a certain way. We may start by loving or caring out of a sense of duty or responsibility but will then find that this grows into a genuine liking for the person concerned.

Of course this may be difficult and it will certainly be costly. It may involve being rejected and even made fun of, and retreat away from love or hitting back in any way is not part of love. It is an enormous task, yet anything else is less than fully Christian. The more that we love, the better people we shall become. The greater, the deeper our friendships, the closer we come to God.

Many will say 'But this is impossible. No one can live up to this'. The expectations only arise as part of a 'love affair with God'. Certainly Christianity *does* demand tremendous things which few people even try to live up to. Thus Jesus says:

> I tell you, love your enemies and pray for those who persecute you, so that they may become the sons of your Father in heaven ... Why should God reward you if you love only the people who love you? Even the tax collectors do that! And if you speak only to your friends, have you done anything out of the ordinary? Even the pagans do that! You must be perfect – just as your Father in heaven is perfect (Matt. 5:43–48).

It is an incredibly difficult challenge, but not an impossible one. It is something at which we can all at least make a real attempt. The question is whether we ever try to take it seriously. If we have really tried with passion and conviction, then we will find it becoming easier. If we have not tried at all, have we any excuse?

The second commandment given by Jesus is, 'You shall love your neighbour as yourself.' For the Christian, the most important thing in life, the centre around which life revolves, is a lived love relationship with God. If this is the centre, then really loving others should involve trying to bring them to this same relationship. Of course it will mean feeding them if they are hungry, clothing them if they are cold and giving to them in need. If we are genuinely detached from the things of this world, then giving away one's material possessions and living a simple life in order to care for those less fortunate than ourselves is really not much of a sacrifice. We are not letting go of that which is most important to us. To wish to build up our possessions and wealth whilst the money could be applied to those in need will come to seem like a contradiction if we are really detached from the things of this world.

This is one reason why much 'prosperity theology' is such a travesty of the truth. It gives the impressions that God's interests and man's material success can go together. It justifies the view that we can be loyal to *both* God *and* the things of mammon. Nothing in the New Testament writings justifies this (although a few isolated quotations can be pulled out to support the position – as almost any position can be justified by texts taken out of context); nothing in the teaching of the Church supports this position and nothing in the writings of the major witnesses to Christianity who have suffered, lived and died for their faith argues for this position.

Prosperity theology is the attempt by those in the affluent West to justify their own affluence and greed and to attribute their financial success to God. It is the attempt to make Christianity comformable with the world. It is the religious life made comfortable and has nothing in common with the suffering, the passion, the commitment and the absolute love of God to which the Christian life aspires.

To continue to endorse prosperity theology whilst hundreds of millions starve, whilst brutal political regimes oppress poor people or those who disagree with them throughout much of South America, Africa and the greater part of the rest of the Third World, while the selfishness of western nations enforces on poor countries continued poverty and human misery through an economic system that the West controls, is nothing short of a scandal. To actually believe in a God who builds on individual prosperity and excess in the West whilst leaving the rest of mankind in squalor, disease and ignorance degrades God. It is a position that arises from self-interest and self-concern and could only have come from within Western religious outlooks. To even attempt to hold the position whilst living amongst the poorest of the poor makes the position almost comical – if it was not so tragic.

Prosperity theology and those who justify it are marvellous examples of the reinterpretation of Christianity into 'religion'. For anyone who feels this attack to be extreme, I would invite them to visit the ghettos of South America, to talk to the dedicated workers who live there and who love the people (not to those who merely visit from the cities); to sit and listen to people who have been tortured for the sake of Christ or who have shared the degradation of the lowest levels of humanity with them – and then to ask these people what they think of prosperity theology.

Indeed, it is not necessary to go outside the West. They can go to Britain's northern cities or to many areas of London, to decaying inner-city Chicago – to the high-rise blocks of flats or the areas where unemployment is above thirty per cent and despair reigns. They can talk to the young drug addicts and teenage prostitutes and watch the misery and hopelessness on their faces. If they can then return to their comfortable prosperity and can still feel that this is the will of the loving God, then so be it. They are free, they must take their own decisions and abide by the consequences – as did Dives!

The little old woman whom I pass in the evenings near Oxford Circus, clutching her carrier bags which represent her world and clad in her many layers of rags which only partly keep out the cold, on her way to some warm grating where she may spend the night in the open, is as much the object of God's love as are the affluent, well fed priests and church leaders or the wealthy farmers or city stock brokers. All of us may be equally far from living up to Christ's call, but the call is to all of us equally and anyone who dreams that the little old woman is less likely to be sitting with Jesus after she dies has not begun to understand Jesus' message. As I pass the little old lady, going back to my warm and comfortable house and good food, I indict myself.

The indictment is made even worse because Jesus told his followers that they were to find him in the poor and the outcasts of society. When I ignore the little old lady and her needs, I am ignoring God. Of course, one person cannot solve the problems of the world – but it is all too easy to move from saying this to saying that there is really not very much we can do at all. We have to be willing to care where we can, we must be genuinely compassionate and interested, even if this is costly to ourselves. This is *not* just a question of financial giving. Indeed, giving money to people in need can be a substitute for real compassion. It can be relatively easy to write a cheque and to feel that we have 'done good'. Just as important is to treat people as human beings whom we care for and in whom we are interested. Money is not the most important thing in life and we can often do far more good and communicate God's love far more effectively by really caring for people as individuals – listening to their troubles and being interested in the difficulties they face.

A friend of mine when she was a novice in a convent used to spend a day a week with the tramps in a shelter in London. She came back smelling rather unpleasant to the convent as she would sit talking to the tramps and really treating them as individuals. When a tramp called at the convent, she would invite him into the kitchen and give him a sandwich and sit down and talk to him. Most of her fellow Sisters disapproved and she was soon forbidden to bring tramps into the kitchen. She would then sit outside on the pavement with them while they ate the sandwiches she made for them.

In another case, a priest with a parish in a smart area of London was asked by the police to stop giving food to tramps as there had been complaints by residents in the neighbourhood that the tramps 'lowered the tone' of the area. Wrongly, in my view, he agreed and tramps were no longer allowed to call. It would have been better to stand out against the complacency of the wealthy residents, even if this had made the priest unpopular – a stand on principle is sometimes required and the principle that individuals matter much more than the 'tone' of a neighbourhood should, for a Christian, be indisputable.

The more secure and comfortable we are, the easier it is to delude ourselves into thinking we really care and we are really compassionate – or at least 'we would be if the need arose'. The need is there all the time; not just with the poor but with the lonely, the unhappy and the insecure. It can help to hold a mirror up to ourselves and to see ourselves as we really are. When we die, this may be done for us and we may have to face up to our reality – to see ourselves and our past actions and omissions, stripped of pretence. I fear that in my own case I will not like what I see. Jesus' call is:

1) to place God at the centre of our lives, to be 'in love' with God so that our relationship with Him is the measure against which the whole of the rest of our life is tested, and

2) to love our neighbour as oneself – in other words to treat all around us as if they were true friends whose interests we are prepared to put before our own, provided only these do not interfere with 1).

If any of us really love God, then everyone needs to be recognised as equally important – without regard to wealth or status. God wants each individual brought to know Him and to love Him. This is an enormous challenge, but the Christian is called to just this; to be a midwife of faith, to draw others closer to God whilst not 'getting in the way'.

The person whom we dislike, whom we find 'angular' or hard to deal with should be welcomed as a further opportunity to show love or to exercise restraint. Anyone who finds Christianity 'easy' or 'comforting' cannot have seen the challenge with which they are faced. Every person we meet can provide us with a chance for showing love and it is easy to put a foot wrong and, by action or inaction, to turn them away from God. This is one reason why it is such a frightful responsibility to call oneself a Christian as, if one does, many people will judge Christianity by reference to our lives. It can be worth looking at ourselves to see how we measure up!

If you imagine a young and innocent man or woman who comes to you because he or she had heard you were a Christian, would there be some aspects of your life of which you were ashamed, which you would not want to reveal to such an innocent? They might be things that your smart and sophisticated colleagues and friends would accept as part of the normal world, but would innocent eyes look at them in the same light? Might these actions of yours not be regarded with surprise and disappointment, as if the young man or woman felt let down that you, if indeed you think of yourself as a Christian, acted in such a way?

Being a Christian is the most difficult thing in the world. I am constantly amazed that anyone dares to call themselves one if they are not trying to live the love relationship with passion and dedication.

Jesus recognised the dangers that one person faces if he or she corrupts another, perhaps by some thoughtless or 'clever' phrase or word. Thus he says:

If anyone should cause one of these little ones to lose his faith in me, it would be better for that person to have a large mill-stone tied round his neck and be drowned in the deep sea (Matt. 18:6–7).

We have a responsibility for others whom we meet in our day-to-day lives and this responsibility needs to be taken very seriously. Complacency about ourselves is, firstly, almost certainly unjustified and, secondly, hides our inability to recognise and live up to our responsibility for others.

True friendship and love have much in common. The Christian is called to be 'in love' with God and to centre his or her life on God, but also to love and care for everyone they meet. This means treating as friends not just those to whom we are naturally attracted, but everyone – even those who are cool or indifferent to us.

9

Soul, Sex and Sin

He: *Do you think you've got a soul? If so, where is it?*
She: *What do you think it means for you to be a person?*

In the United States, concern has begun to be expressed about the young generation whose lives seem to be dominated by television, the Walkman stereo and sex. Increasingly, young people do not read or even think for themselves – instead they depend on external stimulae from television or from the earphones of their stereos. Few enduring relationships are formed and casual sex is acceptable. When people think about relationships, it is often a matter of thinking how to get out of them. Even when two people get married, they first plan their divorce settlement, just in case the marriage goes wrong!

Many peoples' lives have become so concentrated on external diversions and entertainments that they cannot bear silence, they dislike being alone and constantly seek new stimulation. This may result in them seeking more and more material goods (the bigger stereo, car or more expensive clothes) or even drugs. In a real sense, they are losing their individuality, they are no longer fully human. In religious terms, they could be described as losing their souls.

It is not clear what it means to talk of my having a soul. There are two main theories:

1) My soul is a 'separate something' that somehow exists within me. When I die, it is my soul that survives, leaving the outer husk of my body to be buried or cremated. The 'real me' does not need a body. Human beings are different from animals as we have this separate 'soul' and animals do not.

2) To talk of my soul, is not to talk of a different part of me but rather to refer to my humanity. Thus someone might say, 'Peter Vardy has no soul – he is cold and indifferent'. (I hope they don't say that – but they may do!) To say this means that I am not a full person, caring for others and relating to them as fellow human beings. Instead I may be accused of just 'doing my job', acting out my role in life with no compassion and no feeling.

A civil servant might thus be described as 'having no soul' if she turned herself into a machine – acting like a robot. Imagine a social security office: a mother arrives in distress because her husband has left her and she has no money for her children's food. The civil servant who sees her may be official and efficient, the forms may be filled in, the woman told to wait and a decision given. The official's attitude is 'correct' – but no more than that. A machine could have done the same job, and a machine has no soul. The alternative would be the civil servant who cares for the woman in difficulties as an individual. She smiles, sympathises and understands. Possibly advice is offered and alternative sources of help suggested. She is responding as a human being, with understanding and compassion. The whole attitude is different.

Whichever of the above two views are taken, what matters is our development as full human beings so that we become not like machines, but full persons who care and love. Sometimes hardship and troubles can help us in this process – there is nothing like going through really hard times ourselves to help us to understand others. Some South American theologians say this – they say, 'It is all right for you in the West to look at our poverty and suffering and tell us what we should do, but you do not live with us, you do not share our burdens or our troubles. Do you really care?'

In the Middle Ages, some people (such as St Thomas Aquinas) thought that man and every type of creature were created by God with their own nature. The nature of each animal varied but man was distinctive as not only did he have an animal nature but he also had a soul or a spiritual nature. A lion who kills a deer is acting according to its nature and there is nothing wrong or evil about this. Similarly a viper which kills a child is not evil, because it is acting according to its own nature.

After Darwin and our understanding of the theory of evolution, we have come to understand that many animals have evolved from others and, over a long period of time, the 'nature' of animals may change. Nevertheless human beings have had an essentially similar nature for thousands of years. We do have an animal nature – we need to eat, drink, reproduce, keep warm and so on – but we are more than just animals.

If man is merely an animal, then all we have to do is to examine our animal nature in order to understand how we should act. Today, for instance, some evidence suggests that about one in ten adults has a genetic make-up that indicates they will be physically attracted to people of the same sex. In other words they have homosexual tendencies. Now clearly our genetic make up is not under our control – we cannot help our genes. If, therefore, homosexual tendencies are due to our genes, these are part of our nature.

In some circles, there tends to be confusion about attitudes to homosexuality. A person cannot help being physically attracted to someone else – it is what is done with this attraction that is at issue. Homosexual inclinations are

not in themselves wrong. Promiscuous homosexual practices with a number of partners, however, are unquestion-
ably wrong – just as promiscuous heterosexuality is wrong.
The moral problem is confined to whether a long-term
homosexual relationship with another person is permissible. There is no problem in a heterosexual relationship
within marriage – can any parallel be justifiably drawn
with a long-term homosexual relationship?

One answer to this is to simply say, 'homosexuality is
wrong – the Bible says so.' This, however, just will not do
– the issue is more complex and needs greater thought.
Simple solutions are always attractive, but that does not
mean that they are always correct. The Bible prohibits
eating pork as well as usury (lending money at interest).
Muslims still recognise this command and refuse to have
bank accounts or to lend money on the basis of interest
payments. Most of us in the West, however, eat pork saus-
ages and have a building society account. This is not to
say that homosexuality is right or wrong – simply that the
issues are less straightforward than sometimes appears and
they merit careful thought.

It is one thing to have tendencies in a certain direction;
it is another thing to give expression to those tendencies.
Should we, in other words, practice homosexuality as part
of a long-term commitment to another person if we are
inclined to do so by our genetic make-up? We cannot help
our tendencies but we can choose to give expression to
them. Much is going to depend on what we consider our
nature to be.

One way that moral evil was defined (by St Thomas
Aquinas) was to see it as man choosing to 'fall short' of
his true nature. To the extent that we choose to be less
than God has intended, St Thomas considered we were
failing to realise our true potential. If this approach is
going to work, we need to be clear on what it is to be a
human being, what our true nature is and for what we are
intended.

When many people talk of 'sin', they give the impression that Christianity involves a series of strict rules that we must abide by. Failure to keep these rules means that we must feel guilty. In some Churches, the rules are so numerous that a person ends up feeling guilty almost all the time. This can happen particularly in the sexual field. Clergy in some Churches are unmarried and some of them can view sexuality with some suspicion. I know of several women brought up in a particular Church environment where they had very great difficulty coming to terms with their sexuality and ended up feeling guilty at any fulfilment of their sexual nature.

For women, this problem is particularly acute. The one traditional female figure in Christianity is Mary – a Virgin mother. *Not* an easy role for a woman today to live up to! What is more, she is meant to have been an 'intact virgin' even though married to Joseph. For Mary, therefore, there was no question (according to Church teaching), of an active, enjoyable and healthy sex-life. None of us can know what 'the facts' of Mary's sexuality actually were but to hold that she was an intact virgin (i.e. with hymen undisturbed) even after the birth of her Son, makes Jesus' birth bizarre (the idea behind this is that the baby Jesus came through the intact hymen into the world just as the resurrected Jesus came into the closed room without having to go through the door). Mary is hardly a person with whom the twentieth-century woman finds it easy to identify – at least in this aspect. There is no historical evidence for this belief; it was an idea that gained ground some hundreds of years after the New Testament period. Nevertheless in some Churches it is accepted with little question. As another example, St. Cecilia – the patron saint of music – is meant to have told her husband on her wedding night that she intended to remain a virgin.

Sex, it is sometimes held, is intended primarily for the procreation of children. It is not meant for enjoyment independently of this purpose; hence the Roman Catholic

Church disapproves of artificial birth control (the so-called 'safe-method' is acceptable) as this implies a separation between the physical act of love-making and the possibility of having children. If we combine this picture with unmarried priests in the Catholic Church, then questions do get raised as to how we should see ourselves as sexual beings. How should we regard our bodies and our natural instincts?

The view of 'sin' as breaking rules is a feature more of the religious than the Christian centred life and it is an approach that Jesus specifically rejected. The Jews had been given the ten commandments which are very sensible rules for living – but they had not rested content with these. The pharisees had reflected on the teachings of the Old Testament prophets and had, in the Jewish Law (or 'Torah'), built up a very strict set of rules and regulations. These rules were detailed and complicated and it was almost impossible for anyone to follow them exactly.

If, therefore, the Jew measured himself against the law as set out in the Torah, he would always be a failure. He could not live up to the demands of the Law. If he really tried to do so, he would become totally concerned and preoccupied with obeying rules. The letter of the Law came to kill the spirit that lay beneath the law. The Gospels are full of examples of this. Jesus walked through corn fields on the Sabbath with his disciples who plucked ears of corn. They were accused by the teachers of the Law of breaking the Sabbath rules. Jesus replied that, 'The sabbath was made for man, not man for the sabbath'.

The purpose of the Sabbath rest day was to benefit man; it was not meant to be a burden for man and to add to his guilt complexes. Again, Jesus was accused of healing a person on the Sabbath day and was condemned for this. In the story of the good Samaritan, a priest who passed by the wounded man would not help because he was on his way to take a service and would not have been in a state of ritual purity – for him, the ritual laws came before caring for a fellow human being. Again, as in so many cases, the Law had destroyed the spirit that lay beneath it. Jesus continually showed himself to be 'for' human beings – he was not negative and never attempted to lay unnecessary burdens on people.

Christianity calls us into a love relationship with God. It calls us to centre our lives on God and to be 'in love' with God. On this basis, 'sin' is anything that gets in the way of our relationship with God. It is any event, thought or action which interferes with this relationship. This can be both liberating and demanding. It is very demanding in that *anything* that gets in between us and God needs to be rejected and avoided. This is not to deny that most of the old 'rules' and 'don'ts' are excellent guides to conduct and show us which actions to avoid. Stealing, lying, adultery, avarice, gluttony, greed, selfishness, etc. are all going to get in the way of a relationship with God. Jesus' approach is also liberating, however, as our lives need have only one centre and one objective – to draw nearer to God and to care for and love our fellow human beings. As Jesus said, 'My yoke is easy and my burden light.' If only we will take it seriously, following God *does* become easy because all the cares and worries of the world fade away and take second place. They are put in their true perspective.

Anything that gets in the way of our relationship with God needs to be avoided. This is probably something that we have all experienced if we have tried to pray and to come nearer to God. If we really do this and if we try to make God the centre of our life, then we will try to be aware of God's presence with us all the time. Once this is experienced, it is a wonderful presence – it is a growing and increasing experience of the love of God. It is a growing feeling of being loved totally, being accepted as we are and being completely secure. If we do something that we know is wrong, however, then our awareness of God is suddenly made much more difficult. How can we be open to God when we are aware that we have done something, or are still doing something, which we know that God would consider wrong?

It is not so much that God is sitting there with a judgement board and saying, 'You've just broken another school rule – that is one more black mark against you'. Someone could only take this approach if they have never experienced the love of God. Rather it is a feeling of hurt and separation caused by the fact that we have chosen to move away from the light. We have decided, in one or more cases, to ignore God and to turn in on ourselves. To the extent that we have done this, our relationship with God is spoilt.

God's love for us is unconditional – it is there whatever happens and whatever we have done. The Church used to talk of 'mortal' sins – but no sin is truly mortal. Whatever terrible thing we have done, hidden away and not discussed or spoken about, God still loves us. This seems incredible, but this is what real love is about. Most human love, of course, is not like this.

The more I talk to people about their love for other human beings, the more this love seems conditional. They say that they love someone tremendously, but this love is based on certain conditions or on their own interests – it is based on the person loved behaving in a certain way. Our love is partly selfish and if our interests are undermined, then we say that we no longer love. True love, however, is where we really put the interests of the person we love in front of our own – they matter more than we do. If, therefore, they do something that hurts us, this should not really affect our love for them. We should try and see things from their point of view, we should care for them and do whatever we can to help repair our relationship with them.

We are much more than our animal nature. We are destined for a love relationship with God that will begin here and continue after death. To see ourselves only in terms of our animal natures is to debase ourselves. To think that we should just act according to our instincts is to make us no different from a dog or a rat. We are vastly more than this. We have the ability to make choices. This does not mean that our animal nature must all the time be rejected, but it does mean that our physical needs and desires should *not* dominate us or decide for us what we should or should not do. If our instincts are put in first place, this inevitably means that our lives can no longer be centred on God. If, however, we retain God firmly at the centre, then physical pleasures are not wrong – they only become wrong if they 'get in the way' between us and God or if we cannot recognise them openly in our relationship with God.

The Christian is called to live his life as if permanently in God's presence. It is as if God was an unseen observer of our every moment, our every conversation and our every action – not like some 'spy in the sky' but as our dearest and closest friend. When we sin, we shut God out, we turn away from Him and are no longer children of the light. Almost invariably, if an action is right then it can be public property (although this does *not* mean that something is right just because the mass of people approve of it). Once we have to become secretive about our actions, this can be an indication that falseness had crept into them. Ps 19:1–3 puts it this way:

> *Blessed are those whose way is blameless:*
> *who walk in the law of the Lord.*
> *Blessed are those who keep his commands:*
> *and seek him with their whole heart;*
> *those who do no wrong,*
> *but walk in the ways of our God.*

True peace comes when we 'seek God with our whole heart' – to the extent that we put other objectives before this, we will be dissatisfied and we shall be in sin. This should not be a cause for a morbid attitude to life. It is just this sort of guilt-ridden approach that can lead some people to consider Christianity to be a miserable rather than a joyful business. If we turn away from God, we are losing the greatest joy and peace that is available to us, and the real losers are ourselves.

Each of us must decide, before God, how we should act. The least we can do is to ask ourselves, while on our knees trying to relate to God, whether a particular action will draw us nearer to Him or push us further away. Anything that drives us away from God *must* be avoided and rejected. Our sexuality need not fall under this heading, but it may easily do so if allowed to run unchecked.

Assume a woman is married and feels very attracted to another man. There is nothing wrong with really caring for another human being – indeed the Christian is called on to care for everyone. If, however, events get out of control and she has an affair then she is putting herself in a false position. Firstly and most importantly she is putting something in between herself and God. Her life is no longer centred on God, since she has allowed the other man to come first. She will find it increasingly difficult to pray and to be aware of God's presence since whenever she makes herself aware of this presence she is reminded of the falsity of the relationship she has entered into. We cannot open ourselves in love to God and still continue with actions which we know interfere with this relationship. On top of this, of course, the woman's relationship with her husband is being undermined and spoilt and harm is being done to the man with whom she is having the affair. If she really cared for him, she would not place him in a false position.

The affair may continue for a short or long time and God may seem to move further away. God, of course, has not moved – but when we do something that gets in the way of our relationship with God it is we who are choosing to move away from Him.

It is not, however, just the obvious 'sins' that we need to avoid. In fact, so much prominence is given to these 'don'ts' that the underlying purpose of avoiding them is missed. *Anything* that gets in the way of our loving God or *really* caring for all those around us must be avoided. It can be just as much of a 'sin' to be cold and indifferent to people; to treat people as 'objects' who do not matter; to fail to really care for those who are in need or in difficulties; to be selfish with our possessions or to seek our own interests, as it is to commit adultery.

If two people meet, are drawn to each other, really care for each other and a brief affair takes place, I have a feeling that God will look more kindly on the individuals involved, provided the rest of their lives show love and compassion for others, than he will on the upright priest who is always 'good', always does the right thing and never actually loves or cares for the people he meets.

Somerset Maugham has a marvellous short story, *The Judgement Seat*, which expresses this. A man and a woman marry young and, a few years later, the man meets someone whom he falls head over heels in love with. He realises that his marriage is no more than cool. He is an upright and religious man, however, so he parts from the woman he has found and whom he loves very deeply and refuses to see her again. He and his wife throw themselves into missionary endeavour – convinced of how holy and good they are. In fact, the bitterness that has been caused by the affair-that-never-happened turns him and his wife cool and cold not only to each other but to all around them. They die and come before God – sure of their holiness and of their reward, and God is not in the slightest bit impressed. They have failed to love and have turned into sanctimonious and self-satisfied puritans. God has no time for them.

It is all too easy to become cool and cold and to turn away from others. Sometimes a marriage may encourage this. Jealousy is common and one person in a relationship may be insecure and unsure of the other so that, say, the husband denies the wife contact with others; he warns her against developing friendships and insists that the marriage relationship must be the only 'true relationship' – the only relationship that goes beyond the superficial. This, however, is a distortion and a betrayal of love and trust and it is, indeed, a sin as it affects not just the person who is jealous but also the woman – turning her inward, making her cold and preventing her from developing real friendships or relationships. It is not only a denial of and restriction on her personality but also affects the husband as he permits the cancer of mistrust to grow.

We need to recognise that Jesus lived with prostitutes, tax collectors and sinners – perhaps he found more real love amongst these people than he did among the upright clergy of his time. There is a world of difference between talking about being a Christian and living a compassionate Christian life. The latter is vastly more important – we shall be judged primarily on our actions. As Kierkegaard puts it, 'As you have lived, so you have believed.' Our beliefs are best shown in our lives and the way they are given expression. This is the true measure of our commitment. None of the above is in any way meant to imply that, say, adultery and similar 'sins' are right, but just to make clear that we must get things in proportion.

The Greek philosopher, Aristotle, thought that, at first, each of us was free to become good or bad people. In all the small actions and thoughts of our life, however, we are making choices about the sort of person we are. The more we act wrongly, the more we choose to turn away from the light, the harder it becomes to put things right and to turn ourselves back onto the right track again. John Wesley faced this problem even after his conversion. In his journal he says:

In this state I was indeed fighting continually, but not conquering. Before, I had willingly served sin, now it was unwillingly, but still I served it. I fell and rose and fell again.

The New Testament recognises this. In Matthew's Gospel, Jesus says that we can be saved from our sins. In other words, God can save us from the effects of our sinful behaviour. He can help us to 'turn ourselves round', to re-orientate our lives towards God. It was only when John Wesley turned fully towards God that he found the strength to overcome sin. The further away from God we have turned, the more difficult it is to come back – but we *can* always come back. God's love is freely available and his hand is always held out to us. Forgiveness is a matter of re-establishing our relationship with God. If we have never known what a relationship with God means, seeking God's forgiveness means recognising the things that we have done wrong in the past and coming to terms with these so that we can seek God.

Sometimes in the past God has been seen as a great judge in the sky with a large score-board, noting down all our wrong actions and determining that we shall be punished for them if we do not say that we are sorry. This is, however, a totally inadequate view and God's forgiveness is not like this. God came to earth out of love for us. He wants nothing more than that we should really love Him. Talk of punishment is out of place. We are free, however, and if we choose to ignore God, to turn away from God, then that is our choice. God leaves us free to respond or not – as we wish. We must also take the consequences of this refusal of love. It may, indeed, result in endless exile from God and possibly the worst thing after death may be to see our life as it really was and what sort of people we decided to make ourselves. We may find ourselves excluded for ever from God's presence and may realise that we regret the choices that resulted in this exclusion. The worst of it may be that we may come to realise that we brought it on ourselves.

If, therefore, we have led a life that ignores God, we need to set out to re-establish our relationship with Him. The real change that is required is in ourselves. We need to bring ourselves before God, as if before our Father, and to say 'Sorry'. There is no doubt of God's forgiveness *but* we must truly recognise that we are sorry and we must truly wish to turn ourselves round. We must be willing to invest everything we have in the enterprise.

Sometimes it can help to express our sins out loud – to tell someone else about them. In some church traditions, this is done by means of confession to a priest. Even in the Catholic tradition, however, fewer and fewer people go to confession. This is largely because of a failure by the Catholic Church to express clearly what is happening when a Catholic goes to Confession. A young friend of mine went to confession for the first time at her Convent school. She did not know what to confess and was in some distress because she had to think of sins to confess and really did not think that she had been that bad. In fact, she became very distressed about the whole business and, in the end, her teacher had to supply her with a list of sins to confess. When, nervously, she went into the confessional she came across a priest who she afterwards said she thought was uninterested. She really did not know what was happening! Another teenage boy was forced, physically, by his parents to go to confession. It is small wonder that fewer and fewer people see going to confession as essential and, in the case, of the boy, that he has turned his back on religion.

Having said this, however, it *can* help to confess our sins to someone else. It can help us to come to terms with our own mistakes. We often bury the worst things that we have done so deeply that we are hardly aware of them. It can be a tremendous help to sit down and set out those things in our life that we really regret. Of course, it is frightening to express these out loud to another person – but if we can do this to another human being, at least we can be sure in our own mind that we have really recognised our failings before God.

Some churches have a general confession whereby, during the service, the whole congregation says they are sorry for what they have done. This is fine, but because it is so public and so brief we can say the words without ever actually recognising those things in our life that get in the way of our relationship with God.

The crucial point, therefore, about sin is that it should be looked on as any thoughts or actions that get in the way of our relationship with God. We are all sinners as we all, constantly, do or think things that we regret. Every day, if we look back over our life, we will see opportunities to love that we did not take, opportunities for compassion ignored, thoughts and actions that showed a deliberate turning away from God. Christianity calls on us to try, try and try again but, when we fail, does not condemn but helps us to get up and try again.

It follows that the self-righteous religious people who 'tut-tut' in disapproval at some member of the congregation who 'breaks the rules', who turn people away with their attitude or their coldness or who feel pleased with themselves at how good they are, have not begun to understand what Christianity involves. Their lives are centred in the religious – not the Christian. They have not yet found God; they have merely found the security of a religious group.

Christianity does not demand that we succeed as we struggle to love. It does, however, demand that we passionately try to love and to care. We will fall flat on our faces in the mud time and time again. We will look at ourselves and be horrified by what we see. Our past record of failure may disgust us. We may be full of remorse – indeed feeling remorse and regret at our past actions may be an essential part of the journey to God. It is a recognition of our humanity, of our failure. Once we really see ourselves as we are, we have nowhere to turn but to God. *Whatever* we have done, God's love for us is unchanged. All that He asks is that we should be genuinely sorry and genuinely distressed about our failures and that we should seek to turn ourselves around and, once more, to try again.

Robert the Bruce of Scotland was hiding in a cave to

avoid the English armies. He thought of giving up the struggle, but changed his mind because he saw a spider in the corner of the cave. It tried to spin a thread across the corner – and failed. It tried again – and failed, yet again – and it failed. Eventually the spider succeeded and, so the story goes, it was from this that Robert the Bruce coined the expression: 'If at first you don't succeed, try, try, try again.' The same applies to us. However many times we fail, however disgusted we may be with ourselves in retrospect, we must pick ourselves up and 'try, try and try again'. God will always forgive our failures and will always support our renewed efforts *if* we feel remorse and *if* we are really trying with passion and commitment to turn towards Him and to be human beings who can love.

We are more than animals – we have the potential to be spiritual beings who can love and care for those around us and we are intended for eventual fellowship with God. Moral and religious rules are useful guidelines and give us sound advice, worked out over centuries, as to how to behave. Christianity, however, is not a matter of rules and regulations. It rather calls us all into a relationship of love with God and to care and compassion for those around us. Anything that turns us away from God is a sin and we need to restore the relationship by seeking forgiveness. Because God loves us so very much and accepts us as we are, this forgiveness will always be available – but only if we are genuinely sorry, only if we are making a wholehearted effort to turn ourselves round towards God.

10

Suffering and peace

He: *Christians often seem to feel guilty for just being human. I'm no saint, but I don't see why I should feel guilty for being a normal human being.*

She: *For once we agree! Taking Christianity seriously will involve suffering, but not the sort you are thinking about.*

Think of your friends – those you know casually and those you know at a deeper level. How many are at peace with themselves? How many do you think are happy with their lives and face the future with confidence?

In the West, many people take refuge in alcohol or tranquillisers, many others are lonely and the majority of marriages are unhappy. About forty per cent of all marriages end in divorce. To these need to be added the number of couples 'staying together for the sake of the children' and those where love is dead but the partners continue to live together because anything else appears less attractive still. On this basis, the percentage of marriage 'failures' would probably be between seventy and ninety percent. A friend of mine reading this as a draft commented, 'You paint a pretty depressing picture!' I wish it were less so! Life is wonderful, the world is full of joy and beauty and nowhere more so than in our relationships with others. Nevertheless the rate of marriage failure *is* high and many people are, indeed, unhappy.

People focus their lives in different ways – the initial

search for pleasure tends to disappoint. When we are young, pleasures are intense and disappointments are dramatic. As many of us get older, so expectations are reduced. Most people would say that 'we are happy enough in the circumstances'. In reality, many see little alternative to their humdrum existence. They have no real centre for their lives and they see themselves gradually ageing, grey hairs and lines appear, stomach muscles sag and, although it is seldom thought about, loneliness, futility and death lie ahead.

Many people will, of course, say, 'Come off it, it's not as bad as that' – the trouble is that in many cases it is worse. People conceal their real selves from each other – and even from themselves. Few of us have real friends to whom we can open ourselves fully, with whom we can be as we are with no barriers at all. We build up an identity around ourselves to protect us like a cocoon and to ensure that we appear attractive in our own eyes. Often the protection is so good that we avoid looking at ourselves in any serious way as to do so is not very pleasant.

The people who appear happiest are often those who have a purpose or objective outside themselves. For some it is their children – but children grow up, take off and must be allowed to fly from the nest, leaving a vacuum behind. They cannot be held, they must be allowed to make their own lives and parents who try to hang on to their children find the children resentful and rebellious and drifting even further away. For others, the main purpose or objective is their job – they throw everything into their career. Their job gives them identity. All their efforts and thoughts go into making a success of their career. For many, this can bring long-term satisfaction as it gives meaning and purpose to life. It carries respect from colleagues and friends and the person feels that he or she is an important and worthwhile member of society. Dedication to a career fills the hours, provides companionship, direction and purpose as well as, sometimes, a feeling of achievement and excitement.

Obviously our job or career is important, but it can also lead to disillusionment. Too often, the individual is not appreciated and seldom gets thanks or recognition for his or her efforts. A friend of mine worked for forty years as a forester for a wealthy landowner. He worked on after his retirement until he was about sixty-nine. Just before Christmas, the owner's agent came in and said that he need not bother to come back after Christmas – they would let him know if he was wanted again. So much for a lifetime's work! Of course, he has been paid – he had had his due; but the sense of human worth, of a job well done, of having contributed something worthwhile, was missing.

The company that a person works for may get into difficulties and the individual may lose his or her job; promotion that was hoped for may not take place, there may be a takeover and many employees may be made redundant. Even if none of these occur, retirement comes eventually. The more a person invests in his or her job, the more difficult retirement can be. Suddenly the person's identity (which was founded on the employment) disappears. The years stretch ahead without plan or purpose and the search has to start for hobbies to fill the waiting years.

We are back to the question of how we choose to centre our lives. Pleasure fails, the job or career often provides much satisfaction but, in the end, disappoints and you are back on your own. It is the same when we come to die – we always die alone. Death has to be faced by each of us as individuals. Of course, friends and relatives may be around, but in a real sense we are alone. It is our life that is drawing to a close and the pain and the fear is all our own.

It is partly a choice between 'inner' and 'outer'. The broad alternatives are as follows:

1) An 'outer-centred' life – in other words a life centred
   on some external objective. Examples include a life
   dedicated to job, career, success, reputation, money,
   or hobbies. The religious life would also fall under
   this heading as the person is interested in the externals of religion – attendance at Church services, meet-
   ings and similar gatherings rather than the inner
   relationship with God.

2) An 'inner-centred' life – a life where meaning and
   purpose are found within you. The moral and the
   Christian lives are the prime examples under this
   heading. The individuals who are truly seeking to
   live a good, moral life or the person who is trying to
   live out a relationship with God both belong under
   this heading. Both look for the meaning and purpose
   of their lives within themselves.

   The Christian anchors his relationship with God
   in quiet prayer, in times when he or she can be alone
   with God. Even Jesus needed these times. It is like a
   bridge across the river of our day. It is never possible
   to spend our whole day aware of God's presence, but
   just as a bridge has pillars in the river bed which
   support it, so our day needs to have periods in which
   we relate ourselves to God and thus find the strength
   to span the rest of the day. The relationship we find
   with God is hidden and inner, just as the support for
   the bridge is out of sight where it makes contact with
   the river bed. Both give the support needed for the
   part that can be seen.

The 'inner-centred' life will provide meaning and purpose
no matter what happens. If our life is concentrated in the
'outer', in the world outside, we will find our life constantly
affected by things which we cannot control. So many disappointments and periods of unhappiness come from external

circumstances. If we will only look for the meaning of our life within ourselves, the position is different. External factors cannot really affect us. Whatever happens in our job, whatever our hobbies may be, whatever the external circumstances *nothing* can take away the commitment to that which is found within. The New Testament puts it this way: 'Nothing can separate you from the love of God which is in Christ Jesus'. The possibility of a relationship with God is available to each of us, and it is something that we must look for within ourselves. We do not measure this relationship by what happens externally but by the inner transformation that takes place when we turn ourselves around towards God.

A young man I knew was an assistant editor in a publishing firm. I once asked him what his objective was in life. He said that he wanted to be a commissioning editor – commissioning books from authors – and his objective was to be the best commissioning editor in his field in the country. He was seeking for a goal in the outer world and took no account of the inner. Shortly thereafter his firm was taken over, he was made redundant and his dream collapsed. Michael Fairless, the Anglican mystic, in the book *The Roadmender* published in the late nineteenth century, describes life as a roadmender in charge of a small section of country road. The roadmender had to break stones, fill in holes in the road, cut the hedges and generally keep his section of road in good repair. He described the people he met who passed along the road and it is clear that he had an effect on them. His objective was not to be the best roadmender, but to live the Christian life.

Commissioning editor or roadmender – it is not our task in life but the sort of person we make ourselves and the effect we have on others that is important.

The humanists or atheists who do not believe in God can also find a meaning and purpose within themselves – in their case, however, it is not God that they seek but 'the good'. They try to live a moral life and the only reality that they accept is a moral ideal. There is no life after death and no God with whom a relationship may be possible. It must be accepted that this is a noble and admirable point of view and the Christian cannot prove that it is wrong. Indeed the Christian would be right to admire and look up to the person who is truly trying to live this 'good life'. The Christian, however, will still want to hold that something is missing – the sense of God's presence and His love and care; the sense of a fellowship with God and of a life lived in relationship with God. All these depend on being willing to accept that Jesus is, indeed, God and if this step is not taken then the 'good life' will be the limit.

If we try to live the Christian life, seeking God within ourselves and in other people, and becoming more and more aware of His presence with us at all times, then this will transform our lives. The first commandment will, indeed, be first and the second commandment will be almost equally important. Each and every person we meet will be seen as a 'child of God' and we will be able to find God in them as well.

The life dedicated to a relationship with God, however, is likely to lead to opposition and, indeed, suffering. It was not for nothing that Jesus told his disciples to take up their cross and follow him:

> Whoever loves his father or mother more than me is not fit to be my disciple; whoever loves his son or daughter more than me is not fit to be my disciple. Whoever does not take up his cross and follow in my steps is not fit to be my disciple (Matt. 10:37–38).

Some people centre their lives on their children. Their life is given meaning by earning money for their children, educating them as well as they can and, even when the children are grown up, still being involved in their lives – helping and directing them financially and in other ways. Such parents may well be good people, looked up to, respected and admired by colleagues and those in their community. They may go to church and even be church-wardens or church council members. They will probably live in a nice house and have successful children, but they have decided to invest their lives in their children and not in God. They have taken a decision – and the decision is against what Christianity is really about.

Living the Christian life involves detachment from things of the world and investment of everything in the treasure of great price. The suffering that the Christian life involves is not, however, the unavoidable suffering brought by illness or old age. This happens to everyone and people can bear the pain, inconvenience and unpleasantness in different ways. It is also not the frustration of unfulfilled ambitions in the outer world (the failure to become the best commissioning editor). Many think that when the New Testament talks of 'suffering' it is the suffering of unavoidable pain and illness or failure to achieve material success – but this is not the case.

Suffering for Christ is voluntary suffering, freely and willingly undertaken – out of love. The suffering may fall under any of the following headings:

1) Suffering will come because of the opposition and rejection from the world. If we are truly living the Christian life we may have to stand out from the crowd, refuse to compromise and make a stand for what we believe – even though almost all those around reject the view. Charles Mackay, in a robust poem, put it this way:

> *You have no enemies you say?*
> *Alas! my friend, the boast is poor;*
> *He who has mingled in the fray*
> *Of duty, that the brave endure,*
> *Must have made foes!*
> *If you have none,*

> *Small is the work that you have done,*
>   *You've hit no traitor on the hip,*
>   *You've dashed no cup from perjured lip,*
>   *You've never turned the wrong to right,*
>   *You've been a coward in the fight.*

If we stand up for what we believe, if we are prepared, gently but firmly, to take a stand by following God and trying to live out the love relationship with God, we are bound to find opposition. Living Christianity has never been popular. Living 'religion' is a different matter – people understand and tolerate those who just 'go to church' (or chapel), but those who really take Christianity on board and live it in their daily lives are in a different category. They will be considered 'odd' and 'extreme' and this is not an easy burden for anyone to bear. It is much easier and safer to be 'one of the crowd',

2) Suffering will come because we fail to live up to the relationship with God. If we have truly placed God at the centre of our lives, if we are 'in love' with God, then we will all find that we fail to live up to what this relationship requires. We know – or should do – what is needed from us, but we fail to put this into practice. So often we know the good we ought to do but we are simply not strong enough to do it. The Anglican ASB in the Confession expresses this as follows:

> Almighty God, our heavenly Father,
> we have sinned against you and against our fellow men,
> in thought and word and deed,
> through negligence, through weakness,
> through our own deliberate fault . . .

In our relationship with God and in our dealings with our fellow men we should, if we are trying to take Christianity seriously, be full of remorse and regret for our failures. These failures should cause us real suffering – we are so weak and we fail so often. Of course, God loves us and will forgive us but only if we *genuinely* regret our past actions and really do feel sorrow for our mistakes. 'Prattling through' a general confession hardly amounts to genuine regret. Our failures to live up to the love relationship should cause us real suffering as we realise the extent of our inability to respond to God's love.

This is not to suggest that the Christian will be wearing a hair-shirt all the time and going around being depressed and miserable. It does, however, mean that we should take our failures seriously and face up to them. *Once we have done this*, once we have brought them to God, then God's forgiveness is assured and past failures can be left behind us and we can turn to the future.

3) If the relationship with God and love of our fellows are the most important things in our lives, then we will want to share this with others. Few people, however, want to take Christianity seriously – most will quickly dismiss it and get on with the business of 'enjoying life'.

If God exists and if Jesus was, indeed, sent by God, then this is the most important thing in the world and if people fail to recognise this, any Christian will be concerned and troubled. Once again, suffering will occur due to this failure to bring others to see what a relationship with God involves.

If you know something exciting and extremely important and if no one will take any notice of you, then surely you will be in distress? If you really care for the people who are ignoring you, the distress will be even

greater. Somehow you may feel that it is your own
example that is at fault, your own inability to show the
truth of Christianity in your life. This may well be partly
true, although there is a limit as to what one individual
can do for another. One may try to lead another towards
the truth of Christianity – one cannot make the horse
drink!

There is, therefore, a price to pay for Christian commitment and it will often be a high one. Even today, being a
Christian can lead to persecution, torture and death. In
the Soviet Union, Christians find it difficult to get jobs and
have been sent to prison or hospitals for the insane. In
South Africa, tens of thousands of Christians are behind
bars or banned due to their commitment to their fellow
men, leading them to oppose the government. In many
countries in South America, Christians are taken out and
shot at night or simply 'disappear' because they put their
commitment to God and their love for the poor who suffer
under oppressive regimes before their own lives. In China,
in spite of recent liberalisations, becoming a Christian
means standing out against the rest of Chinese society and
rejecting ideas which go back thousands of years and which
are deeply embedded in the Chinese psyche. In many countries in Africa, Christians are helping the poor and deprived
and risk death in doing so.

The same story has been heard throughout the history
of the Christian Church – suffering and opposition has
always been present when people try to follow Christ. In
Western Europe and North America we are fortunate in
being free, but the danger is that this freedom may be seen
to mean that Christianity is no longer costly. If this
happens it is because 'Christianity' has been transformed
into 'religion'.

Jesus told the famous story of two men who built houses
– one built on the sand and the other on the rock (Lk.
6:47–49). The person who built the house on rock had a

much more difficult building job to do. Foundations would have had to be cut into the rock and it would have been a time-consuming business, but his house, when finished, was secure. Similarly if we base our life on God – if our foundations are inner – then in spite of the difficulties that may arise, nothing will be able to shake us, our lives will have found a security, a love and a meaning which is possible nowhere else.

Following God will always be costly. It will involve challenging the existing order and rejecting the commonly accepted way of looking at things. As an example, Western Europe and North America are immensely rich in comparison with the rest of the world. This is not just a coincidence, nor is it a matter of the West working harder. The whole world economic order is dominated by the West and this domination is exercised to its own advantage. Multinational companies ensure, by many means, that real wealth comes to the West and as little as possible is kept in the Third World. Such companies are, rightly from their point of view, serving their shareholders – they are maximising profits and increasing dividends. The price for doing this is, however, often massive Third World poverty.

Just as it was Christians who first stood out against slavery and rejected the accepted norms of their society, just as it was Christians who first stood out against child labour and rejected the norms of their society, just as it was Christians who first stood out against racism and rejected the norms of their society so we, in turn, may be being called to be the first to stand out against an economic order which benefits us most of all and which almost everyone around us accepts without question. A lead is necessary, a lead which puts the interests of others before our own, a lead which requires love.

Today, we look back on the days of slavery and wonder how people who called themselves Christians could take part in the slave trade – but they did. Today, we look at South Africa and see the main Afrikaans Churches supporting apartheid and fail to understand how they can possibly justify this – but they do. Tomorrow, people may well look back at our generation and wonder how we could have tolerated a world in which there is such inequality of wealth, such institutionalised poverty in the Third World – yet most of us accept this with little question and those few who do not are regarded as 'outsiders' to mainstream religion and somehow 'extreme'.

Although Christianity can be costly, the peace that goes with a relationship with God completely overwhelms the external opposition. To know that we are loved by God and are trying to show this love in our lives, to know that we are trying to serve God and that *nothing* (not even death) can separate us from God, is the greatest gift in the world. Someone who is really taking Christianity seriously will find a peace that can be found nowhere else and this peace may be seen by others. There are some people who, when you meet them, exude an almost tangible peace and gentleness. This is probably the best 'advertisement' for Christianity today – it is like a light, a beacon which will beckon others on. Regrettably, it is all too rare.

Danger and falsity come when any of us think that we have found God and no price has been paid. If our life is successful and comfortable and all is going well for us, if we go to Church every week and are popular and respected, the chances are strong that we are a long way from the kingdom of God. As Jesus says:–

Happy are you when people insult you and persecute you and tell all kinds of lies against you because you are my followers. Be happy and glad, for a great reward is kept for you in heaven. This is how the prophets who lived before you were persecuted (Matt. 5:11–12).

Everyone will hate you because of me (Matt. 10:22). So do not be afraid of people . . . Do not be afraid of those who kill the body but cannot kill the soul, but rather be afraid of God who can destroy both body and soul (Matt. 10:26 and 28).

This is not to say that being hated by the world is something that necessarily follows from being a Christian. What it does mean, however, is that we must be careful not to regard popularity as any real indication of how well we are relating ourselves to God. To measure this, we need to look at ourselves as if in a mirror – we need to look at our true selves, which will probably be well hidden from those around us.

We have to choose to centre our lives in the 'outer' or the 'inner'. Only in the 'inner' is there true freedom, only here is real security which is not dependent on external factors beyond our control.

If we really try to follow God, we will face opposition and will suffer from not being able to be understood. Suffering will come from having to stand out against the crowd; from our own failure to live up to what the relationship with God requires as well as our inability to bring others to see what the inner life involves.

On the other hand, the person who is truly trying to live a Christian life will find a peace and calm which is available nowhere else. He or she will find the love of God, which exceeds everything that can be expressed in words.

11

Community and Church

He: *'You are nearer to God's heart in a garden than anywhere else on earth'. You don't need to belong to a Church to be kind to people.*

She: *Agreed, but there is more to it than being kind to people. I thought I had made that clear!*

We belong to different communities – to the village, neighbourhood or street in which we live; to union or trade associations; to school organisations; to clubs or societies; to the community of our family and, perhaps, to a Church. A church is a community. People and our relationships with them are essential to finding meaning and purpose in our lives.

In any reasonable size town or village there will be many different churches – Anglican, Baptist, Catholic, Congregationalist, Reformed, special evangelical Churches and perhaps even an Orthodox Church. Nearly all, however, would regard themselves as forming part of the catholic Church. Now I can well imagine the horror that some people might feel at being branded as 'catholic' – a Northern Ireland Protestant is hardly going to take easily to being told she is a catholic! Much, however, depends on a capital letter. There is a world of difference between 'Catholic' and 'catholic'.

In Britain, the Catholic Church (with a capital 'C') is often called the 'Roman Catholic Church'. This is not always a popular title amongst Catholics who have traditionally liked to consider that there is one, true Church – their own. Since the Second Vatican Council in 1966, however, the Catholic Church has recognised that there is truth not only in other Christian denominations but even in other religions. The true meaning of 'catholic' (small 'c') is 'universal' and *all* Christian Churches are members of the one, universal, Christian Church. This is why the Apostles' Creed says:

> I believe in God, the Father almighty,
>   creator of heaven and earth.
> I believe in Jesus Christ, his only son our Lord . . .
>
> I believe in the Holy Spirit,
>   The Holy catholic Church . . .

Entry to this one, universal (catholic – small 'c') Church is by baptism. There is no such thing as an Anglican, Catholic or Methodist baptism – rather there is Christian baptism. Once baptised as a Christian, re-baptism does not take place. There is some difference in approach by those Churches who believe only in adult baptism. They maintain that infant baptism, when babies cannot decide for themselves, is inappropriate and they would therefore seek adult baptism so that the individual can make his or her own, mature decision to join the Church. In those Churches which practice infant baptism, they also seek a mature and formal entry by the individual and this takes place at Confirmation. Nevertheless in spite of Confirmation, it is the baptism that is considered primarily important.

One possible long-term solution that has been suggested to the problems of Northern Ireland, where two communities face each other with different Church labels ('Protestant' and 'Catholic'), might be to move towards an ecumenical, Christian baptism so that all children were

clearly recognised as being baptised as *Christians*. This
baptism would then be recognised on both sides of the
sectarian divide. It is an excellent idea and there is no
theological reason at all why it should not go forward,
although there is great resistance to it from both sides of
the Northern Ireland community. Neither side likes to face
up to the fact that they are Christians – they prefer to see
themselves adhering to particular religions ('Catholic' or
'Protestant'). Many people in the province (as elsewhere)
centre their lives on religion rather than on God. If their
lives were truly centred on God, then the suspicion and
violence between the communities simply would not occur.
The problems arise, however, when both sides of the divide
identify themselves not with God but with a Church.

The same problems occur with mixed marriages
between, for instance, Catholics on the one side and Anglicans, Baptists or Methodists on the other. Great strains
can be set up in the marriage by the Catholic's closed
attitude to other Churches, especially when the non-Catholic is banned from the Communion table (this, to me,
always seems slightly strange as the Communion table is
sometimes described as the 'Lord's Table', and yet it is a
Church which bans many Christians from this). Again,
this view comes from putting adherence to religion before
love of God. One of the great strengths of the Anglican
and other non-Catholic churches is that they welcome to
their communion table all Christians, no matter what
Church they belong to. This openness is, surely, the attitude that Jesus himself would have endorsed.

It is not for nothing that the Apostles' creed links
together the Holy Spirit and the universal, Christian
Church. The different Churches all feel themselves guided
and influenced by the Holy Spirit – in other words by God
Himself. To be sure, many Churches in the past have done
terrible things which Christianity is totally shamed by.
Burning heretics, the work of the crusades and intolerance,
lack of compassion and care has been a feature of Church

history. God is often ignored by the Churches and, today, it is recognised that the demands of a Church alone cannot be allowed to decide issues – each of us must make the final decision ourselves. We can and should, of course, listen carefully to the views of any Church that we belong to but, at the end of the day, obedience to individual conscience rather than a Church reigns supreme.

Christianity believes in the importance of each of us, as individuals. It believes that every one of us is tremendously valuable; that God loves us – not simply because we are part of a mass of people, but individually. It believes that we are free and will have to render account for how we have lived and the sort of people we have chosen to become. God's love is personal. Christianity also believes in the importance of the community of the Church. What, then, is the function of the Church?

First of all, we need to recognise that, when it comes to a decision between the importance of an individual and the importance of the crowd of people making up the Church community, the individual will always come first. This is one of the crucial distinctions between Christianity and Marxism. By contrast, Marxism considers the mass of people to be more important than the individual. It may frequently be necessary for groups of individuals to have to be sacrificed in the interests of the long-term destiny of the mass of humanity. This attitude can lead to slave camps in Siberia – the individual is less important than the state. Marxism's objective is the long-term happiness of the mass of mankind here on earth at some time in the future. This will be brought about by historical forces which the Marxist considers are inexorable and are certain to be overwhelming. Marx was strongly influenced by Hegel, and Hegel saw forces at work within history moving mankind forward to steadily greater heights over the centuries. Marxism looks for the overthrow of capitalism by the triumph of the power of the workers. As part of this historical development, some individuals will have to pay the ultimate price and lose their freedom in the interests of the State.

For Christianity, the individual is of paramount importance. Christianity's objective is to bring each individual into a personal relationship with God which begins here on earth but continues after death. This cannot be done by any emphasis on numbers. Each person must be brought to an individual decision and each of us is tremendously valuable and important. Any Church which loses sight of the importance of each of us is not faithful to Christ's teaching. The Church is made up of individuals and, in Christianity, individuals come first.

Christianity has been described as the purest form of communism. The first disciples held everything in common. Thus:

> The whole body of believers was united in heart and soul. Not a man of them claimed any of his possessions as his own, but everything was held in common, while the apostles bore witness with great power to the resurrection of the Lord Jesus. They were all held in high esteem; for they never had a needy person amongst them, because all who had property in land or houses sold it, brought the proceeds of the sale, and laid the money at the feet of the apostles; it was then distributed to any who stood in need (Acts 4:32–35).

This first experiment in communal living did not endure. We are individuals and must take individual responsibility for our lives – not only before God but also in terms of our survival. As we have seen, if we are Christians we will be detached from the things of this world including material possessions. We will love God and our neighbour and if our neighbour is hungry, cold or in need then we will not want to hold onto our possessions but will be anxious to share them. The Christian will, therefore, want to give and to share – out of love for others. No Christian would ever seek to force other people to do likewise. Persuasion and example would rather be used. The Communist maintains the need for all goods to be held in common, but this is done forcibly. Pure, theoretical communism would have everyone sharing equally. The way communism has been applied in practice is very different from this. A privileged élite soon emerges who have access to most of the perks and possessions enjoyed by the previous rulers.

It is not surprising, therefore, that some theologians have sought to develop a form of 'Christian Marxism'. The real question is whether God is placed at the centre or man. If God is placed firmly in first place, then the term 'Christian' may be appropriate. If, however, the first commandment is abandoned in favour of the second, then what remains is not Christianity.

Only a minority of people today consider that, when it comes to drawing close to God, it matters which Church we belong to. God is greater than the barriers we impose between ourselves. The Bible constantly shows God's love extending beyond the supposedly 'chosen' people (Naaman the Syrian is healed, Elisha goes to the Shunemite woman, the Roman Centurion has greater faith than any in Israel, Jesus heals the Canaanite woman's daughter, the Samaritan is the true neighbour). The result is that almost all Churches work closely together – either through the World Council of Churches (where all major Christian Churches, except for the Roman Catholics, are represented) or through more local arrangements. The Catholic reluctance to participate at a formal level in the W.C.C. may owe more to historical claims to being the 'one true Church' than to the modern, post-Vatican Two spirit which pervades most aspects of the life of the Church. Each Church has its own identity and this identity is important.

The differences between the Churches at a theological level are significant (at least to theologians and priests) – but at a deeper level the Churches share far more than that which divides them. It is rather like differences within a family – there are differences between members of the family and at times tensions can arise between family members, but the fact remains that all the members belong to one single family. Too often in the past the Churches have forgotten this and it is to their shame that they have not shown a greater desire to move together, to understand the viewpoint of the other and to concentrate on those things which unite rather than the much less significant divisions.

Baptism marks the entry of an individual into the world-wide, universal Christian community but also into the particular Church community in which the baptism takes place. At a local level, the particular church members will often welcome the new member to their community and this is one good reason why a baptism in the middle of a service is an attractive option.

Some Church communities emphasise baptism as an entry point into their own community rather than into the wider Christian community. In so doing, they perpetuate the divisions and tensions between the communities. Northern Ireland is, again, perhaps the classic example – an individual is looked on as either 'Catholic' or 'Protestant' – rarely simply as a Christian. There is a tendency by some Churches to move away from an emphasis on propositional beliefs which have guided them in the past and to substitute membership of the Church community as the central condition for membership of their Church. This may well be right, but it is the wider Christian community that they should see themselves as belonging to and into which new members are baptised – not simply the community represented by their own denominational label.

Is baptism, however, required in order to love God and our neighbour? The Churches might maintain that baptism was instituted by Jesus himself and they are following his directions. This is true, but this is not to say that it is *necessary* and *required* to be baptised in order to know God.

A Roman Catholic colleague of mine told me of her school days and how, when she was a young girl at school, there was a Jewish girl in the class. Her class mates were obviously concerned that this girl had not been baptised – so they proceeded to carry out the ceremony for her, under the sink tap in the cloakroom. The girl wanted this to be done and had learned about Christianity in her school lessons. The school authorities were then told – and they were horrified. Authorities were consulted higher up the hierarchical ladder, and it was confirmed that the baptism was valid and had to be accepted. This may well be the case in Catholic Canon Law, but to say that God's attitude to the (formerly) Jewish girl was altered as a result of the cloakroom tap does seem a bit far fetched.

I can imagine that a reader of this paragraph might say that I am being gratuitously critical. This is not my intention. Jesus did, indeed, affirm the importance of baptism. Baptism is the way the Church marks entry into the Christian community and it is a central ritual and sacrament of many Churches. These Churches feel assured that, through it, God works. This may well be true, but it does not rule out God working outside the Church. Church membership alone does not bring anyone into a relationship with God. Hitler, after all, had been baptised!

Membership of a Church is, however, very important indeed on the journey towards God. This journey is a long one, lasting throughout our lives. We should be aware, as we continue on the road, of God's presence with us. Sometimes God will be very close, at others we will move far away from Him. The journey towards God is not a simple progression in which we get closer and closer. There will be tests and trials on the way and for days, months or years we may be driven off the path altogether. Jesus said that the road was difficult – it would be a stony and narrow path compared with the broad and wide road of a self-centred and pleasure-seeking life.

If we are climbing mountains, it is wise to go in a team.

The team members can be roped together so that, if one slips, the others can help him up again. So it is with the Christian journey. If we are part of a Church community, joining together in regular worship and sharing with some members our pleasures, joys and difficulties on the road, we can find support and help in the difficult times.

Throughout the history of the Christian Church, men and women have formed communities to live together. Often these have been enclosed and the monastic communities kept learning alive in the West after the downfall of the Roman empire. The Benedictines, Carmelites, Cistercians, Dominicans, Jesuits and others all formed Christian communities with their own rules of life. Some of them are totally enclosed (such as the Carmelites), others run schools (such as the Benedictines and Dominicans), yet others are highly individualistic (such as the Jesuits – although, today, some younger Jesuits are seeking to move the Society towards a greater realisation of the importance of the community side of their life). Whatever their different rules, however, they are all, also, part of the wider Church community.

Today, there are exciting groups of lay people (and sometimes clergy as well) who are coming together to form tighter communities than the normal Church provides. One interesting example of this is the community of Christ the Sower in Little Gidding near Huntingdon in England. Here Anglicans, Catholics, Methodists and Quakers all form part of a single, Christian community. They all have their own accommodation and to that extent are independent, but they also form part of their own community – coming together to worship God, for occasional meals but, above all, recognising that they are part of a single Christian community in which they care for and support each other on their individual journeys towards God.

Robert Van de Weyer, who is one of the leaders of the Little Gidding community, has written a short book (*The Little Gidding Way* DLT, 1988) which gives a sane and practical approach to community living in the late twentieth century. It is not doctrinaire but is realistic and recognises the need for each individual's independence as well as the importance of community. It is a book that many parishes could usefully study if they ever get round to considering what it means for them to be a Christian community in their own place.

We are not alone. We are human beings and we need the care and love of other human beings. Sometimes this is a difficult lesson to learn. It is one thing to be always ready to help, to be always strong and in command – but if we are like this, always in control, we may be less than fully human. Love is a two-way process and sometimes we need to learn to receive love, care and compassion as well as to give it. One of the hardest lessons of all is to be able to accept help willingly and gracefully.

Time and again in my own life, when talking to people about their own spiritual journeys, I have found new insights and guidance. God works through people. In loving people, in opening ourselves to them, we can find God's reality more clearly. The more we turn away from people, the more we turn away from God. We may well find that we go out to someone whom we feel needs help and support and we end up being supported ourselves. We need each other on our journey to God – we need our friends, we need to be sure of their understanding and their love, we need to know that their commitment to us, and ours to them, goes beyond the petty upsets and misunderstandings of day-to-day life. We need to know that our failures and inadequacies will not make them turn away from us.

A living church is a community of people who really do care for, love and support each other, who care for each other as individuals and who can provide strength and support in difficulty. They are then enabled to take this strength out to the wider community in which they live. The members of the church should recognise that they are all journeying together towards God. They are fellow pilgrims on the road of faith and when anyone gets side-tracked from this road or gets stuck, others are there to help.

If a Christian community is successful, there can be a real temptation for the community to turn in on itself and to resent intrusion from outsiders. This, however, is a snare that must be resisted. The opportunity to show others the love of God and to care for them must always be taken. The slight glance of resentment, the coolness when someone arrives as a visitor may do untold harm. It is a luxury that a Christian community cannot afford.

This picture of a caring and loving Church is rarely found in practice. Too often, there are isolated individuals who come together once a week to sing a few hymns and to listen to a rapidly forgotten sermon. The individuals remain closed and refuse to open themselves to each other. I remember when I was working in Johannesburg in 1971 going at Christmas to the Anglican Cathedral and walking out in embarrassment when 'the peace' came. Members in the congregation actually *turned and shook hands with each other!* This has long been a feature of Catholic services, but I had never come across it in an Anglican Church. It required me to 'open myself' and to acknowledge the person sitting next to me, and I could not bring myself to do it. Since then, I have come to recognise the value of this gesture – by turning and shaking hands with the next person in the pew, by smiling at them and acknowledging their presence, we are enabled to feel part of a real 'community of faith' – but this is a step many are reluctant to take. English reserve takes a lot of breaking down!

There are dangers in church membership as well as strengths. If a church is not 'alive', if the members of the church do not really see themselves as on a road towards God, then a Church can be positively dangerous. Priests can be dangerous too! It is not easy being a priest, but too many find that they cease to be ambassadors of God and instead become religious functionaries – ceasing to visit their flocks and ceasing to love those for whom they are pastorally responsible. The priest can be put up on a pedestal in a comfortable, middle class house, with a secure living and a pleasant existence. He is looked up to and admired, his reputation is secure, he chairs many local committees and is a person of power and of consequence in the area. The challenge and demand of Christianity can too easily be forgotten and instead the Church which the priest leads may become solely concerned with 'religion' – more interested in the size of the congregation than the pilgrim's way. If someone comes into this sort of church, then they can easily be given the impression that all that is required is to go to church once a week and to give generously towards church finances (possibly not in that order!)

Sören Kierkegaard described some priests as, 'Prostitutes of eternity'. Just as prostitutes live by selling their bodies, so some priests have a comfortable life and build up a considerable reputation by 'living off' the New Testament – they are secure, unchallenged, independent and happy, having come to an understanding with the world. They serve mammon rather than God. It is a sad but, unfortunately, all too frequent picture. It is a temptation of which all priests should be aware.

There are various symptoms of this. Churches which remain locked all week with only occasional services are one example. There are, to be sure, problems with thieves and vandals stealing from churches in some areas. One of the traditional tasks of the priest, however, was that he should say the morning and evening 'offices' or services, in church, every day.

I well remember a priest called Robert in the little Hampshire village of Selborne where I once lived. Every single morning he was in church at 7.10 a.m. to say his prayers. At 7.30 he would ring the church bell and say the Communion service. Few people came. Twice a week, at

11.00 a.m. he would say the Litany in church and, finally, at 6.30 he would say Evensong, again ringing the bell. He was a small man, but whatever the weather the village would see him walking to church in his black cloak and hat – a living witness to the importance of prayer and a testimony to his faithfulness. He had a considerable effect on the village, but his is an example that few priests still follow. Some would say they are 'too busy' or that they say their prayers in their bedroom – but any priest who says he is too busy to find time for God or that he is too busy to open the church to any who wants to come needs to ask himself if he has his priorities right. Too often priests have turned themselves into social workers – they have placed the second commandment firmly in first place.

What makes a good priest? There are many different qualities and it is certainly not an easy job. Above all, he (or she, in some churches) needs to be a pastor, living with and guiding the church community with love, compassion and understanding. Not judgemental, but ready to identify at all times with those who find the road difficult. A young trainee priest whom I admire said to me recently that, although he accepted that Christianity was challenging and difficult, he could not find ways to put it over in a six minute sermon to the man on a Clapham bus. This particular man is, I know, an example of a dedicated individual who is setting out determined to relate his whole life to God. He understands the difference between the God-centred and the religion-centred life, but also sees the practical difficulties of bringing people to see what a God-centred life involves. The mistake is, possibly, to see the priest's role as something that is apart from and above his flock. The priest needs to live with, to encourage and to bring his flock to God and this is probably done more effectively by indirect communication than by 'preaching at' them.

Traditionally, the Roman Catholic Church was, and still is, monarchical with the Pope at the summit, cardinals next in line, bishops lower down, then priests and finally the mass of people at the bottom of the pyramid. The Anglican and Orthodox Churches, by contrast, have a federal structure with each Church in a certain area being independent and representing its own, individual pyramid, although still part of the worldwide Anglican or Orthodox communions. The leader of each local Church (in England the Archbishop of Canterbury) is but one bishop amongst many – he has no power over the other bishops, although he certainly has great influence. Baptist, Methodist and U.R.C. Churches tend to be more democratic – they are, perhaps, more truly 'churches of the people'.

The Church should not be modelled on the idea of the priest in the lead and the people meekly following. Priest and people are all on the road to God together. They need to support and help each other. Jesus himself said that the greatest amongst the Christians should be the servant of all. He, after all, was God and he came to earth, mixed with the lowest members of society and washed his friends' feet! It is not always easy to reconcile this picture of Jesus with the priest in his robes, with all the attention directed at him, leading his flock.

The future is likely to see a much greater lay involvement in all Churches than hitherto. One of the most encouraging features for Christianity in Europe and North America may be the decline in numbers of priests as this is forcing the laity to take a really active part in the Church. The laity are beginning to realise that *they* are the Church, it is *they* who must visit, it is *they* who must love, it is *they* who must pray, it is *they* who must care. The days of seeing Christianity as a matter of leaving things to the 'professional', who is employed for the purpose, are over. Provided the bishops and Church leaders have the courage to make use of the laity, the future could be exciting with active, involved and outgoing churches made up of all the people.

Having said that priests can be dangerous, the same

applies to the laity. There can be a risk of the people seeking a Christianity that they find comfortable. People do not like to be challenged. They do not like to have to face up to the demands that Christianity really makes. Many want 'both/and' rather than the choice of 'either/or' – they want *both* a happy, prosperous, secure life *and* Christianity as well. They want *both* God *and* the world. Jesus, however, said that a choice was needed – it was a matter of deciding to centre one's life on *either* God *or* mammon. Life, as we have seen, can only have one centre and the attempt to combine God and the world generally ends up putting God into second place.

If the laity is put in control there can, therefore, be the danger of churches seeking the lowest common denominator. No call will be made that is too demanding and the 'spirit of the times' will come to rule. Churches always need renewal – they need to be challenged. Leadership must come not from priests or from the laity, but from God. This, of course, sounds fine in theory, but how does one know what is from God and what is not?

There are dangers in biblical fundamentalism. Texts in the Bible, taken in isolation, can be read off to support many different positions. It really requires an openness and obedience to God, measured against the tradition of the Church and, even more, against the essential spirit of Christianity which is centred and rooted in compassion and love. Anything that is harsh, that is critical, that is negative and judgemental is unlikely to come from God (which is not to deny or reduce the challenge and demand of Christianity). Jesus had a talent for picking out the positive factors in people and building them up – whenever he saw people who were doubtful and unsure of themselves, he had an instinct for spotting their strengths. Evelyn Underhill, in *An Anthology of the Love of God*, puts it this way:

. . . Christ never criticised any but the respectable and

pious: with every one else His thought went like a shaft of delight straight to something He could admire – the love of the prostitute, the meekness of the publican, the faith of the centurion, the confidence of the penitent thief – all things which irradiate and save humanity. Love looks for these first, and one reason why Christ gives us rest is that in His presence we are bound to love – not to criticise.

The test is love – not just passive love, but a passionate love. A love of God and a love of our fellows which refuses to condemn or to judge, which constantly seeks the good and the positive and always rejects the negative and the critical. Some 'religious' people have been turned cold by religion, they have lost the capacity to care for others as individuals, compassion no longer moves them. They are quick to judge and always critical. Such individuals are no guide to God's ways. They have missed the road and need to be led gently back. Their criticism and harshness need to be met with gentleness and care.

We cannot judge others, just as others cannot judge us. Others may see our actions, but even then they may only see part of the picture. They cannot see our uncertainty, our mixed motives, our personal struggles onwards towards the light and our constant set-backs, doubts and difficulties. We cannot and must not judge others, but we do need to be willing to resist and combat harshness, coldness and indifference, we need to be ready to challenge those who would drag others down, those whose influence is wholly negative. Sometimes the challenge is best made indirectly, but always we must be ready to stand up for the person who is being persecuted or criticised, always we must be ready to see the best in people. If we always err on the side of thinking too well of others we are unlikely to go too far astray. Love never judges and never condemns. The marvellous thirteenth chapter of the first letter to the Corinthians puts it this way:

Love is patient; love is kind and envies no-one. Love is
never boastful, never conceited, nor rude; never selfish,
nor quick to take offence. Love keeps no score of wrongs;
does not gloat over other men's sins, but delights in the
truth. There is nothing love cannot face; there is no limit
to its faith, its hope, and its endurance (1 Cor. 13:4–7).

The Church, therefore, should be a help and support to all
of us on the road to God. It is not impossible to come close
to God without ever going to Church, but it is much more
difficult alone. Too often, the reluctance to go to Church
is a reluctance to let the barriers of self down, a reluctance
to put self into second place and to open oneself to others.
It is much easier to stand aloof and alone, convinced of
our own rectitude. The one essential entry ticket that is
required before starting on the Godward path, however, is
to abandon our assurance of our rightness, to recognise
how far away we are from God and how little we can do
alone. Proud and self-confident, we will never get near
God. Ashamed, frightened, unsure and aware of our own
inadequacy we will, if we will only make a small effort
towards Him, find His hands ready to shelter and support,
to protect and lead onwards. It is that acceptance, that
affirmation of love that we *should* find within the Christian
church.

*The catholic (small 'c') Christian Church is the universal church of
all believers – no matter what label they may wear. Each church
community should be a support and help to all its members on their
individual journeys towards God. It should see itself as part of the
wider Christian Church and recognise other Christian churches as
providing a valid path towards God. It should encourage, affirm,
guide, suggest, exhort and comfort and never reject. It should be a
society of people full of compassion for each other and for those
outside – committed to God and to bringing the peace that comes
from knowing God to everyone around them. It should be a source
of strength in trouble and difficulty and always a body of people*

aware of the living and very real presence of God. Sadly, it often does not live up to this picture – but this is not a reason to reject it, rather we are all called to transform it from within and to make it truer to the vision.

12

Fraud

He: It's been a lovely evening and I like you a great deal, but I think you're a bit of a fraud!

She: *I'm glad you like me – the feeling's mutual! But why do you think I'm a fraud? That's a terrible thing to say.*

He: Well, you've put up a convincing case. I can see that Socrates and Jesus must be distinct and, being honest, I suppose I can't see any way that the Christian Church could have grown quite so rapidly if Jesus had not been more than a man. I've always found it incredible how the disciples reacted after the crucifixion. It seems totally out of human character. Their friend and leader had been killed by the authorities, the crowd of Jewish people in Jerusalem had turned against Jesus. The disciples had run away – they were safe and the authorities were not going to chase after them. The logical and sensible thing to do would have been to keep their heads down and to return to their previous jobs, recognising what a mistake they had made.

It really seems too unlikely that they could have made up the story of the resurrection. Who would have believed them if there had not been strong supporting evidence? Also, the Jews or Romans could so easily have produced the body – we know that a guard was set on the tomb.

She: *I'd never really thought of it like that.*

He: All in all I accept that Jesus was radically different from Socrates and, although I don't like the consequences, I accept much of what you are saying about Christianity. To me, it seems odd that so few Christians today seem to take it seriously – many of them appear quite content to go to church, sing a few hymns and not do much more. I think that is one of the things that's always put me off – there's always seemed a gap between what Christianity should involve and the way it is practised. If it's true, surely it must be demanding?

The reason I think you're a fraud is that I've never pretended to be a Christian, whereas you say that you are one. At least I have always been honest in saying that I didn't believe – you, however, have always said you did but I wonder how much difference it's really made to you? Oh, yes you're a nice person – I wouldn't like you so much if you weren't. But you don't measure up to the standard you have set yourself and that you say Christianity requires. You're good at talking about it, but it seems to me not much good at living it. Forgive me! It's probably the wine talking.

She: *I see what you mean . . . I suppose I am a bit of a fraud as you say. I don't like to admit it though, even to myself.*

I do think Christianity is true, I do think it is possible to have a personal relationship with God, I do think trying to show compassion and love is what we are here for and is the only real way of finding peace and meaning in life, but there is a world of difference between knowing these things and putting them into practice.

You might say that I know the path I want to take, but find it incredibly difficult to travel along it. It's so easy to go along with everyone else and be comfortable. The pressures are very great.

Christianity requires us to try, and try with passion and dedication, to seek God and to really love and care for those

around us. I agree that I don't live up to this. But Chris-
tianity does not demand that we succeed – it asks us to try,
try and try again – like Robert the Bruce! Maybe I'm a
fraud because I don't try hard enough. I really do want to,
but it is very difficult sometimes. Jesus said that it would
be. At least I've decided on my path. I know the road I
want to travel but do a poor job about actually going along
it.

What about you, though? What path do you want to go
on? I have a feeling that you don't really want to think
about it. I may not succeed in travelling far along my chosen
path, but you don't even have one.

He: Well . . . it seems to me that, *if* Christianity is true,
          it is the most important thing in the world and
          seeking God is the most important task we can
          attempt in life. I don't much like the alternatives.
          I suppose I have lived the unreflective life. I've
          never really thought much about what life was
          about and have drifted along – happy enough, but
          without any real sense of direction. That's easy.
          The problem you've given is that I have to decide
          between your five alternatives.

          The life of pleasure sounds, initially, to be fun,
          but even I recognise that this will lead to selfish-
          ness. The ethical life has an appeal, but I am not
          sure I'm strong enough to do this. Also, it's a very
          individualistic life isn't it? I think I do need to
          belong to a community, to feel there are others
          (such as you!) who will be there to understand and
          help. I need help from outside and the ethical life
          does not provide this. The religious life seems a
          betrayal of what Christianity should be about and
          I don't think I could persuade myself to believe in
          that.

          So, that seems to leave me with two basic alterna-
          tives. I can either suppress your questions and go
          on as I have been doing, not thinking about the

future, or I have to face up to Christianity. I tell you now that I would prefer the first of these – it's a lot easier! But you've raised the questions, and I can't just ignore them. That doesn't leave me many alternatives does it . . . ? I'm not sure I like this conversation!

She: *Mm, I know what you mean. It's always easier not to think. I suspect there is something in human beings that resists thinking through the deep questions or, if we do, few of us get round to doing anything about them. The trouble is that I really do believe it is all true. I do believe we can be aware of God's presence in our lives – but if I feel like this, why do I find living up to it so difficult sometimes?*

He: Perhaps you're beginning to realise you're human. Perhaps you have learnt something this evening as well. Maybe you are trying to do too much yourself. If God is there, shouldn't you be a bit more trusting? You seem to want to rely on yourself all the time. Perhaps this is your mistake. If God is there and loves us as you say, perhaps the first step is to commit ourselves to Him – I'm not sure you've done that. You want to do it all on your own.

She: *Heavens, at the start of this evening I was so sure of myself. I feel as if I've been turned inside out!*

He: I know, and I hadn't expected this sort of conversation either. There are not many people I can talk to like this . . . You say we must trust, but I wonder just how much you do this. If you go back to the early disciples, they trusted completely. They left their jobs, their families and their security to put Christ first. You've said we've got to be detached from things – I'm beginning to think you may be right, but you're only paying lip service to this. Perhaps you need to take more of a step to doing something about it – you need to show your trust in your own life. If you do this, perhaps real progress on the path you have chosen will be possible.

It's easy for me to talk about you, though. Perhaps it always is easier to talk about these things than to do something about them ourselves.

She: *I think we're good for each other, and I also think you may have a point. Come on, it's getting late. Are you going to give me a lift home?*

He: Of course. It's been a lovely evening – thank you. I wonder whether either of us will do anything about all this talk . . . ?

THE BEGINNING

Detailed acknowledgements

John Murray and Wm. Collins & Co. kindly gave permission for the quotation respectively of three verses from John Betjeman's poem 'Christmas' and for the quotations from C. S. Lewis' book *Mere Christianity*.

This book is not in any way a summary of Kierkegaard's thought, although my personal debt to him is considerable. Kierkegaard is often considered to be an existentialist and is badly misunderstood by many commentators – in fact he was a very committed Christian in the mainstream tradition. He wrote many books, often using pseudonyms, and no one book by itself provides an overview of his thought. (I have, so far, been unable to persuade any publisher that there would be a demand for such a book!) For anyone who would like to explore his ideas further, the following may provide helpful starting points. *Philosophic Fragments* is mainly a book on Christology – in this he compares the figures of Socrates and Jesus. A story similar to that of the 'coalminer's daughter' in chapter 3 is included in this book. *Concluding Unscientific Postscript* deals with the truth of Christianity as being subjective rather than objective and the need for indirect communication. Section 2, part 2 is the most important although it is not easy reading. *Either/Or* contrasts the life of a seducer (representing the aesthetic life) and Judge William, a happily married man (representing the ethical life). *Purity of Heart* is Kierkegaard's outstanding spiritual book and is an excellent aid for personal meditation – it asks each individual to consider whether he or she is really living Christianity (I have used his dedication in *Purity of Heart* in this book). *Fear and Trembling* examines the story of Abraham in detail and its implications. *Training in Christianity* sets out the demands of Christianity and *Attack upon Christendom* is a sustained attack on the established Church and most priests. *Point of View on My Life as an Author* looks back over his own life and reflects on how God has continually educated him into what being a Christian involves. The six volumes of his *Journals* provide useful insights into his thinking. All these books are published by Princeton University Press except for *Purity of Heart*, which is published by Harper and Row.

I am grateful to Sr. Anne-Marie Quigg who, in an essay comparing St Theresa of Lisieux and Kierkegaard, introduced me to the phrase 'living the love relationship'. Professor Stewart Sutherland of King's College, London, introduced me to the story of Jaggerstater. H.H. Price ('Survival and another world' in Donnelly's *Language, Metaphysics and Death*, Fordham University Press 1978) helpfully explored the difference between 'belief in' and 'belief that'.

Various friends have given permission for anonymous anecdotes about themselves to be included in this book.

Biblical quotations are taken from the Good News Bible (Collins and The Bible Societies).

Index

*See also acknowledgements at the beginning and end of the book.

If you wish to receive *regular information* about *new books*, please send your name and address to:

London Bible Warehouse
PO Box 123
Basingstoke
Hants RG23 7NL

Name..

Address...

....

....

....

I am especially interested in:
☐ Biographies
☐ Fiction
☐ Christian living
☐ Issue related books
☐ Academic books
☐ Bible study aids
☐ Children's books
☐ Music
☐ Other subjects